Teaching the Sixties

Ge
T.

Center for Teaching Library
The Westminster Schools
1424 West Paces Ferry Road, N.W.
Atlanta, Georgia 30327

Teaching the Sixties

An In-depth, Interactive, Interdisciplinary Approach

Brooke Workman
West High School, Iowa City, Iowa

Center for Teaching
The Westminster Schools

National Council of Teachers of English
1111 Kenyon Road, Urbana, Illinois 61801

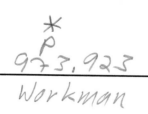
© 1992 by the National Council of Teachers of English. All rights reserved. Printed in the United States of America.

It is the policy of NCTE in its journals and other publications to provide a forum for the open discussion of ideas concerning the content and the teaching of English and the language arts. Publicity accorded to any particular point of view does not imply endorsement by the Executive Committee, the Board of Directors, or the membership at large, except in announcements of policy, where such endorsement is clearly specified.

Library of Congress Cataloging-in-Publication Data

Workman, Brooke, 1933–
   Teaching the sixties : an in-depth, interactive, interdisciplinary approach / Brooke Workman.
        p.   cm.
      Includes bibliographical references.
      ISBN 0-8141-5236-8 (pbk.)
      1. United States—History—1961–1969—Study and teaching (Secondary) 2. United States—Civilization—1945– —Study and teaching (Secondary) I. Title.
   E841.W59   1992
   973.923'071'2—dc20

92-12672
CIP

Contents

Handouts

Preface

Cultures teach us the stories by which we will live.

Frank Smith[1]

In 1958, I began teaching high school classes in Waterloo, Iowa. I taught American literature in the English Department and American history in the Social Studies Department. In both classes I followed department curriculum guidebooks. While some freedom was allowed with daily lesson plans, the prescribed approach was survey-chronological, from colonial times to the present, using well-bound textbooks for a year.

Although wanting my students to share my own enjoyment of literature and history, I felt some obligation to the canon: the "standard" literary and historical interpretations. I felt a concern for what E. D. Hirsch now calls "cultural literacy"—that students know the names and dates and titles, the key lines and quotations and that they should read the classics.

I followed what seemed to be the accumulated wisdom of all those who had come before me. I used their lecture outlines and textbook questions, their worksheets and unit tests, their suggestions for five-paragraph themes and book report forms. And I kept those 140 students seated in straight rows facing my lectern.

This was a familiar pattern with my colleagues, and it was unsettling. By the end of that first year, my students were much like American tourists at the end of a two-week whirlwind tour of Europe—overloaded with souvenirs and largely mixed up about where they had been. They confused or quickly forgot the material that had once given them passing grades!

In 1968, in Iowa City, Iowa, I began teaching American Humanities in the English Department. While the college students at the nearby university were busy with sit-ins and pouring blood on the steps of the Old Capitol, I began my own little revolution. In 1975, I announced it to a larger world through my NCTE publication, *Teaching the Decades: A Humanities Approach to American Civilization.*

But my journey with American Humanities was not over.

In July of 1987, I traveled alone to the Wye Plantation in a remote region of Maryland to join sixty teachers for three weeks of soul-battering at the English Coalition Conference. It was there I fully realized the enormity of our task: to set the course of "English" in American education as we move toward and into the twenty-first century. It was there I also realized that few of us knew each other. And it was there I realized that my work with the interactive component of teaching and learning American Humanities was not over.

Indeed, the extraordinary unanimity that emerged at the end of the English Coalition Conference was due in large part to the interactive process. While the process began in the familiar large-group setting, the dynamic learning occurred in the small groups. It was there, in an atmosphere of mutual respect, that we talked together, wrote together, read together—and even shared our drawings. But what I remember most was that, when things seemed hopeless, we stopped and did freewrites. Then we shared our stories.

Somehow, this process cleared the air and empowered us all.

Home again in Iowa City, I began this handbook on the 1960s. I knew it was time to make sense of this decade. It was time to share our stories that define our American identity.

Note

1. Frank Smith, *to think* (New York: Teachers College, Columbia University, 1990) 63.

Introduction

A Course of Study

Title: American Humanities

Length: One Semester

Grade Level: 11, 12

Description

American Humanities is an interdisciplinary study of American civilization that is designed for students who wish to learn a method of understanding our culture—past and present. The students experience American values and make an in-depth analysis of one historical period.

During the first half of the course, the students develop projects that test their understanding of the process. The content includes literature, history, media, architecture, art, dance, and music. The learning methods include artifact analysis papers, small groups, audiovisuals, field trips, and the project. When the course is over, the students should have a method for understanding and appreciating the American way of life.

American Humanities Questions

Q. What does it mean to be an American?

Q. What lessons in cultural literacy build on the students' prior knowledge and develop a sense of control and understanding of American culture?

Q. How can students become actively involved with their immediate and larger American community?

Q. How can the teacher and the students develop in-depth learning, using primary sources and interdisciplinary materials?

The Triad of American Humanities

Buckminster Fuller, the radical American architect who so impressed his young audiences in the 1960s, built his geodesic dream houses with a sense of the past. He understood the strength of the triangle—the triad that still holds the weight of ancient domes. This handbook is built on theory and practice, on more than two decades of exploring

American culture, on the strength derived from a triad for both teaching and learning:

An

In-depth,

Interactive,

Interdisciplinary

Humanities Approach

In-depth Learning

This handbook presents a sustained study of one decade, the 1960s. But this is no survey course, no chronological course, driven by a textbook and standardized testing of information. As Handout 1 shows, this course goes in deep for ninety days—an intensive study of a dynamic period that leads students to a larger understanding of American culture, to an expertise so rare, and so delightful, in secondary education.

The first handouts reveal a flexible process for achieving in-depth learning. The first section ("The Idea of Culture") invites students to reflect on American values, past and present, before they leap into the 1960s. It challenges them to look closely at their world—the artifacts, the people, and their experiences—and to theorize about all those things that molded them and the world of the 1960s. In doing this, the students become both insiders and outsiders. And in doing this, they have begun to learn a method for understanding themselves and the stories of the American landscape for the rest of their lives.

Handout 1 and the ninety daily lessons that follow also reveal a flexible, in-depth process for studying the 1960s:

1. *The schedule.* The instructor can follow the exact "tentative" schedule or rearrange the specific artifact sections when the students have completed the first two sections, "The Idea of Culture" and "The Historical Period: 1960s."

2. *The lessons.* The instructor can use only the daily lesson, only the alternate or additional suggestions that accompany most of the lessons, or combine the lessons and suggestions.

3. *The materials.* The instructor has great flexibility in selecting the materials—which are largely primary sources—for instruction. The lessons suggest a variety of choices, depending on availability, level of difficulty, and student interest. The lessons are also designed with an eye to the school budget. The teacher can order materials or rely on

available departmental materials, as well as explore the free and inexpensive resources of the school and community: libraries, resource persons, local architecture, and especially the students.

4. *The project.* Finally, the tentative schedule shows that in-depth learning occurs not just through classroom interaction with decade resources and artifacts. During the first half of the course, the students initiate an in-depth project that has a life of its own. This project, which involves ten steps before completion and presentation, weaves in and out of the ongoing decade study. And it is this project—which students unanimously assert is the most important aspect of the course—that reveals authentic achievement. The in-depth project reveals how students, alone or in collaborative settings, create and produce knowledge that has value to their own lives.

Interactive Learning

The configuration—the seating—of the American Humanities classroom is that of the circle. It conveys the message of interactive learning: "We are going to learn together." The in-depth study of the 1960s (or of any other American decade) involves developing and testing theories in a climate of mutual respect for the ethnic, racial, and religious diversity of the participants.

Learning occurs best in open, active classrooms where students are empowered by their own reading and writing, sharing and showing, questioning and examining, creating and performing. While the teacher establishes the climate, activates prior memory, and shares stories of the culture, the students must also teach each other.

Examples of interactive learning are presented in the lessons of each section:

1. *The Idea of Culture.* Students share artifacts of the American culture.

2. *The Historical Period: 1960s.* Small groups develop ten theories about the decade.

3. *Popular Culture.* Students share and defend position papers on popular books and films as decade artifacts.

4. *Architecture and Paintings as Artifacts.* (a) Students work in teams to write analyses of community buildings. (b) Students teach paintings to the class.

5. *Poetry and Plays as Artifacts.* (a) Partners create anthologies of decade poetry and share them in small-group settings. (b) Small groups discuss, perform, and analyze decade plays.

6. *Dancing and Music.* (a) The teacher and students dance and theorize together. (b) Small groups teach the class about music or develop and evaluate lyrics analysis assignments.

7. *The Project.* The in-depth project reveals how students share the knowledge that they have produced alone or in teams. They share the products of authentic learning—from original research papers to creative, interdisciplinary, multimedia responses that have considerable interest to their peers. They teach, they perform, they interact. They reveal their creations that go far beyond mere proving of competence.

Evaluation

Evaluation must be considered an essential part of interactive learning. We all need to know how we are doing, but we all need to be involved in evaluation. We all need consistent and multiple forms of evaluation. And we need a reasonable and humane evaluation system where students are involved in the process.

This handbook suggests a system.

The American Humanities evaluation system begins in Lesson 1. The students are alerted to basic expectations and to an alternative evaluation system: *H* (highly satisfactory), *S* (satisfactory), *U* (unsatisfactory). Each student will have a folder, which will be kept in the classroom. In this folder, evaluations will be recorded by the instructor and by the students.

The folder system will be the basis for the self-evaluation essay at the end of each grading period, when students review their products and classroom performance. The students will translate their products, performance, progress, and personal reactions into the grading system of the school. The instructor, in turn, will review these self-evaluations in factoring the final grade and in considering the necessity of holding conferences with students when disagreement occurs. (Note: My students insist on the the *A–F* system for evaluating the major project.)

Interdisciplinary Teaching and Learning

We all live in an interdisciplinary world, and we all learn life's lessons in context. From birth, from childhood, we learn the facts, the content of this world from many teachers, from many settings. Until we enter a place called "school," the teaching and learning seem very natural.

But when we go to school, we find ourselves in separate buildings, in separate rooms, on separate floors, with people called "teachers." While the interdisciplinary world is always there, we enter another world where teaching and learning are more defined by boundary lines, by disciplines and departments.

American Humanities is based on the concept that life isn't really departmentalized. Human beings cannot escape the variety of their culture, the piecing together of their cultural jigsaw puzzle, the search for what it means to be alive. Of course, students and teachers know all that.

Students instinctively understand that concept. They love variety. They seem to resent the term "content course," which suggests that facts of one segment of the world must be memorized, notes taken, tests scored. Students are delighted by the interdisciplinary variety of content and the heresy of overlap. They know that learning is always about people, about themselves. And so they enjoy the challenge of theorizing about their world, past and present.

Teachers know all these things as well. They are always in search of new ways to prepare their students for the larger interdisciplinary world. No matter what their training or background, they are resourceful and committed to their students. Whether first-year teachers or experienced teachers, they are always in search of flexible approaches to authentic learning.

This handbook was written for those students and for those teachers.

Handout 1

American Humanities: Tentative Schedule for the 1960s

The Idea of Culture

1. Orientation
2. Getting Acquainted
3. Culture and Values in Children's Literature
4. Dominant Values and the Top Ten of TV
5. Heroes, Heroines, and Consensus Seeking
6. Other Cultures and Culture Shock
7. Individual Values
8. Artifact Day
9. Artifact Day
10. Theories and Learning

The Historical Period: 1960s

11. Orientation: Terms and Tentative Schedule
12. Assigned Readings: *Waking from the Dream* or *Coming Apart* or Both
13. Documentary Film
14. Researching Terms
15. Formation of History Small Groups and Activity Commitees (for example, Handbook, Artifacts, Bulletin Board, Media)
16. Reading, Research, Small-Group Procedures
17. History Small Group 1
18. History Small Group 2
19. History Small Group 3
20. History Small Group 4
21. Class Consensus on History; Orientation to Oral History, Date Research, Genealogy
22. History Options
23. Oral History Presentations and Papers
24. Date Research Presentations and Papers
25. Genealogy Presentations and Charts
26. Orientation: Term Projects

Popular Culture—TV, Films, Bestsellers

27. Television
28. Television
29. Decade Films
30. Decade Films
31. Decade Films
32. Orientation: Bestsellers
33. Chunking a Literary Artifact
34. Reading and First Conferences; Proposals Due
35. Reading and First Conferences
36. Reading and First Conferences; Position Papers Due
37. Bestsellers: Defense Day (or Small Group 1)
38. Bestsellers: Defense Day (or Small Group 2)
39. Bestsellers: Defense Day (or Small Group 3)
40. Self-Evaluation Day

Final Test

During the last week of American Humanities, you will select a large envelope containing artifacts. You are to imagine that you are living in the distant future—say 3000 A.D.—and on another planet. You have discovered a time capsule containing this envelope. After you return to your home planet, your anthropology society asks that you present a paper in which you describe the artifacts, theorize as to their meaning, and expand upon your analysis by suggesting what you think this barren planet once had for a culture. You are able to translate the language, though you will know only what the artifacts say in themselves. Your report will be from three to five pages.

Teaching the Sixties by Brooke Workman. © 1992 NCTE. Copied by permission.

Lessons 1–10
The Idea of Culture

Current psychological research supports the view that learning takes place most effectively in an interactive setting where students are encouraged to develop and test hypotheses on their own. Such classrooms focus on what students already know in order to build on it.

The English Coalition: Democracy through Language (85)

Lesson 1
Introduction

Goal

Orientation and introduction. This first day should acquaint the students with the nature of the course. It should introduce them to the method and content. After the course has been taught once, student evaluations can be used to orient and interest beginning students.

Materials

1. The introductory handout (Handout 2), "American Humanities: Introduction."

2. Evaluations of the course from previous classes, if available.

3. A copy of the recent TV Nielsen ratings, which can be found in any newspaper TV guide.

Assignment

Students should bring to class a notebook for keeping handouts and assignments, as well as for response writing and learning logs.

Procedure

1. As you take class roll, ask each student to name a favorite TV program. (Ask the first student to write the others' responses on the chalkboard.) If they don't have a favorite or don't even watch TV, fine. When you finish taking the roll, ask the students why you asked them this question. Note: You have begun the process—talking and thinking about culture.

2. Then ask the students to explain their answers, their choice or no choice. Why is this program a favorite? Why don't some of them have one?

3. As the students respond, ask them whether they see any patterns emerging from their list and their answers—similar favorites, similar content, similar reasons for enjoying programs, often ones that have been popular for more than one year. Why? And why don't some people watch television?

4. Next, with the introductory handout as a guide, discuss why this course is being offered and why it is an important course. Explain that the course will deal with a very important question: What does it mean to be an American? The course will also deal with a more basic question: What does it mean to be a human being?

5. Reassure the students that this course will be both fun and challenging. It will have great variety: literature, history, films, music, dancing, painting, architecture, popular culture. There will be class activities, many small groups, and individual instruction. After ten lessons on American values, the students will study one decade for the rest of the course. Note: The 1960s may be the required decade or a choice for class voting. Also see Brooke Workman, _Teaching the Decades: A Humanities Approach to American Civilization._

6. At this point, describe the methods of evaluation for the course to allay any fears of failure. Suggestion: Evaluation: American Humanities Criteria, an initial multifaceted evaluation, with the accent on self-evaluation, that may be used for the first section or for the entire course:

Evaluation: American Humanities Criteria:

_H:_ Highly satisfactory (strong); _S:_ Satisfactory (okay); _U:_ Unsatisfactory (weak).

	H	S	U
1. Following directions: work done on time	_____	_____	_____
2. Memory of course information	_____	_____	_____
3. Ability to work with others; group roles	_____	_____	_____
4. Understanding of central concepts; ability to apply them	_____	_____	_____
5. Writing skill	_____	_____	_____
6. Effort, improvement, class discussion	_____	_____	_____
7. Attendance	_____	_____	_____
8. Major project	_____	_____	_____

7. Finally, ask the students to write a summary in their American

Humanities notebook of what they have learned today—and to bring that summary with them for the next class meeting. Note: You have now established another key to the process—writing and thinking about culture.

Alternative or Additional Suggestions

1. Seat the students in a circle if the class is smaller than twenty, in two concentric circles if larger. The message of the circle will be clear from day 1.

2. Develop an interdisciplinary concept for open discussion. You could define the course as relating to students' lives, which are made up of parts, but parts related to each other. For example, have the class discuss the students' average day from morning to bedtime, which molds and reinforces values: choice of clothing, the home and school architecture, the people who teach them, their favorite music and books, television programs and films, their motorcycles or cars, their part-time jobs, sports, dancing, art. Students should be challenged with questions: Why is it that the United States is one of the few nations with cheerleaders? Why do you dance the way you do, prefer a certain hair style, when Americans in other decades chose other ways and styles? Are we born with a love of football?

3. Play a popular recording or tape. What does it say about America?

Introduction—The Study of the Past and the Present

Objectives

1. To acquaint students with the interdisciplinary approach.

2. To acquaint students with a vital era of American civilization.

3. To foster individual research based on attitudes of appreciation (humanities), analysis, and objectivity.

4. To encourage students to reflect on their immediate environment as would a cultural anthropologist.

5. To initiate experiments in learning, for example, use of varied materials, student evaluation, committees, individual and group projects (such as an in-depth project), and resources—student, school, and community.

Content

American Humanities seeks to relate the various parts of American life, past and present, and to understand the relationship of the parts to the whole. In the beginning, we shall discuss such ideas as "culture" and "values." We shall recognize that our social heredity is learned from childhood, although we are not often aware of this legacy. As we reflect on the present, we hope to discover who we are; as we study the past—a particular decade—we shall discover who we were. But it will also be apparent that generations are not only different but similar. We shall see shifting attitudes, different cars and clothes, but we shall see relationships between decades in such things as literature and art. We shall see how ideas that began in the 1960s have blossomed today. And as we approach the end of our course, we should be sensitive not only to facts but also to generalizations. This is not just a content course; it is more of a methods course.

As you approach our study, try to set goals for answering some of the following questions:

1. What are the major American values? How are these values— standards of good and bad—transmitted?

2. What are American artifacts? What does each artifact say about American society?

3. What is the relationship among various American artifacts: poems, TV programs, films, bestsellers, paintings, popular music, buildings, dress styles?

4. Is there such a thing as the "spirit" of a time? Was everyone either a hawk or a dove, a member of the silent majority or the counterculture, a straight or a hippie in the 1960s? And just what is the spirit of the present?

5. What does it really mean to be an American? What does it mean to be a human being?

These questions will be approached in many ways—reading and writing about books, watching films, teaching art slides, listening to music, working on a project, participating in large and small group discussions. *But ultimately only you can find the answers.*

Teaching the Sixties by Brooke Workman. © 1992 NCTE. Copied by permission.

Lesson 2
Getting Acquainted

Goal

Introduction of the instructor and the students. This day will be an exercise in humanities. Barriers must be broken down; patterns of friendship must begin. These things must happen because students will be working with each other as well as with the instructor, often in small groups, some on major projects. Everyone must begin to know each other.

Materials: None

Assignment

Students are to bring a children's book—or toy—to class on day 3. Ask them if their family still has these artifacts from their childhood.

Procedure

1. Review Lesson 1, asking the students to read from their humanities notebook about what they learned. Remind them that the course has no textbooks. Therefore, the notebook will hold important handouts, as well as their own writing. For example, they will be asked to keep a learning log during the architecture section.

2. Then begin the lesson by noting that you genuinely want to know the students and to have them know each other. Everyone will be working together in the course. Refer to the idea of the circle in a classroom. What is the significance of a circle in a classroom versus classes where the chairs all face the front?

3. The students and instructor should pair off in twos or threes with people they do not know or know slightly. Without notes, they should interview each other, asking questions that each would like answered— where the other lives, family, job, favorite foods, sports, travels, plans for the future. Such questions often lead to friendships, mutual understanding, and interaction in many of the class activities, especially in small-group activities and projects.

4. After about five to ten minutes, the pairs should introduce each other to the class by conveying what each has learned about the other. Now the class has had its first step toward interaction.

Additional or Alternative Suggestion

Send students to all parts of the classroom. Tell them that there will be no talking during the entire period. But they must communicate with each other through slips of paper that you will provide. (Cut a stack of paper into quarters.) Select two students as messengers who will carry the slips from student to student. The teacher participates, too! Begin: Students write whatever they want to another person, fold the note, address it to the intended person (at first they may have to use a physical description). They signal a messenger to take the note to that person by pointing or by writing a note to the messenger. This process continues through the entire period. Students may keep or throw away their notes. This activity really opens up communication—observation, getting acquainted with classmates and the instructor!

Lesson 3
Culture and Values

Goal

Understanding the concepts of culture and values, especially how values are formed, transmitted, and reinforced.

Materials

1. Handout 3: "Definitions."

2. A children's book or tape. Suggestions: *The Three Little Pigs, The Little Engine That Could,* or any recent children's artifact.

Procedure

1. Give every student a copy of the handout. Stress the idea that certain words will be used throughout the course and that these words must be mutually understood.

2. Read or ask a student to read the definitions for "culture" and "values." Stress that people in various parts of the world, and even in various parts of the United States, are different because they learn different things in their "cultures" and therefore have different ideas about what is valuable or "good." Note that people who travel are often disturbed by the values of other cultures. Ask those students who have traveled outside the United States to relate their experiences. Have the students discuss the cultural diversity in their school and neighborhood.

3. Then note that the values of a culture are acquired in childhood, often through reading and listening to stories. These are artifacts—refer to the handout definition. Play or read a children's story—an "artifact," an object made by humans in a culture for the children. Ask the class to take notes on values that they hear being taught to children. Then ask them to share their notes for open discussion.

4. For example, *The Three Little Pigs* is really about people, mothers and children, and about such American values as hard work and practicality. There is a concern for success and a kind of humanitarianism, as well as a blend of individualism with conformity. The wolf, a morally evil force in the story, is now becoming extinct because it has been

stereotyped as a bad animal. Students will suggest many other values and will enjoy the humor, if not the nostalgia, of these stories.

Additional and Alternate Suggestions

1. As a lead-in to the study of the 1960s, you may wish to use print and tape versions of the stories of Dr. Seuss or the poetry of Shel Silverstein.

2. A videotape of a TV children's cartoon—with advertising—can be valuable to develop these concepts. Remind the students of what they and their brothers and sisters have watched. Invite discussion of how and why children—and teenagers—are targeted and manipulated by commercial interests.

3. An important alternative or extension of the concept of childhood and values is the study of toys. Encourage the students to bring these artifacts to class—baby dolls, Barbie dolls, cars, trucks, airplanes, G.I. Joe, space toys, computer games. Ask the students which doll should be given to a male or female child—or should a child be allowed to choose? Discuss how sex roles are taught, how the 1958 Barbie doll created a revolution. The baby doll (even the "anatomically correct" one) was replaced by a sexually developed "sister" who, by the 1970s, was more concerned with dating, shopping, and partying with her twenty-one friends, including Christie (1968), Julia (1969), and Brad (1970), who were African American. What values were being stressed in the toys of the 1960s?

Handout
3

Definitions

Culture

Culture is a continually changing pattern of learned behavior and the products of learned behavior (including attitudes, values, knowledge, and material objects), which are shared and transmitted by the members of society. Culture means:

1. That the behaviors of people are largely learned
2. That they are organized into patterns
3. That these patterns result from the teaching (conscious or unconscious) of other people
4. That they exist in the form of both material objects and intangible thought-habits like attitudes and knowledge
5. That they tend to be somewhat uniformly shared by members of a society, learned from and taught to each other largely unconsciously
6. That these ways of doing and ways of thinking make up the pattern of human lives
7. That these ways are constantly changing

Society

Society may be thought of as the organized group of people who enact a culture. They constitute a group of people who have lived together long enough to become organized and to consider themselves a unit.

Values

Values are ideas that contain or express prevailing estimates that people have of their relative worth or importance of things. Americans often express values in terms of money, but we also value success, beauty, a high standard of living, democracy, speed, and education. People within a culture—or a subculture—have their own special values. For example, by the 1950s and 1960s the American "teenage" subculture emerged with its own heroes and artifacts that revealed values quite different from those of adolescents of previous generations.

Attitudes

An attitude is an orientation of "tendency to act" in some way toward some person or situation or object or idea. Stated simply, attitudes amount to likes and dislikes, attractions and repulsions, interests and apathies. Sometimes they are covert or hidden or masked. They are learned gradually; often they result in stereotypes or caricatures. The controllers of the media try to shape our attitudes. Many of us have conflicting attitudes toward the same object; this is called ambivalence.

Social Class

A social class is any portion of a community marked off from the rest by social status—prestige, esteem, honor, power. A ranking system exists in most cultures, even in American society, where much lip service is paid to democracy. Status determinants vary, but often include wealth, education, sex, race, religion, nationality, occupation, lineage. The 1920s, for example, has been called the age of the rise of the middle-class American.

Artifact

An object made by human beings in a culture.

Lesson 4
Dominant American Values

Goal

Understanding dominant American values.

Materials

1. Handouts 4 to 6: "Dominant American Values"; "Assignments—Values Transmission and Reinforcement"; "Model Student Artifact Analysis of a Popular TV Program."

2. On the chalkboard: The Top Ten Television Programs, according to a recent popularity poll, such as the Nielsen Poll, which can be found in recent newspaper TV guides.

3. (Optional) A videotape cutting of a popular TV program, past or present.

Assignment

Students should copy the Top Ten Television Poll. They should select one program to analyze: (1) Summarize the plot. (2) Identify the dominant values in the program and in the sponsor's advertising by giving examples. Most students should find at least eight values. They should be given a week so that they can study the program they wish to see. DUE: _____ .

Procedure

1. Summarize the previous lesson on culture and values, especially those values transmitted through stories and toys.

2. Note that television is a major means of transmitting values for everyone from children to adults. Refer to the class poll on favorite television programs in Lesson 1. Ask the students to describe the favorites of their parents and other adult family members and friends.

3. Give each student a copy of the dominant values handout, as well as the assignment sheet and the handout of a student TV artifact analysis (Handouts 4 to 6).

4. Ask the students to copy the Top Ten from the board. Describe the assignment, especially as an exercise in finding values that large groups of Americans accept.

5. To help the students understand the assignment, do not simply read the list of values aloud. Instead, ask the students to think of major American heroes and heroines, past and present. Then go around the class, asking the students to volunteer names for a chalkboard list. After about thirty names—one per student—are written on the board, ask each student to look at the handout and find a value that matches the hero or heroine. Place the value beside the name. Some names will have more than one value. Remind students that not all heroes and heroines are admired by everyone, nor are they all law-abiding. American folk heroes include Jesse James or even criminals such as Bonnie and Clyde. And not all are real people; we have fictional heroes, media heroes, too—from Superman to Rambo.

6. Ask the class to decide on one person as the most admired by Americans. What values does this person represent?

7. Finally, ask the students to examine the model TV artifact analysis (Handout 6).

Additional and Alternative Suggestions

1. Instead of making a list of American heroes, ask each student to name someone he or she really admires. Place all names on the chalkboard. Then go back and ask each student to identify the value or values that fit his or her choice. Next, ask the class to do a subculture analysis of this list: What are the major values that prevail in their class list? Is it a sexist, racist list—a list limited to certain occupations and lifestyles? Did they mention family members?

2. Remind the students how heroes can be identified: faces on coins and stamps, names of schools and public buildings and streets, statues, even names of children at birth. Does any student have a name of a hero or heroine?

3. Ask the students how values can conflict. Remind them that value conflict, ordering of values by priority, and both liking and disliking a value (ambivalence) often occur in America. Discuss our ecology, where science, material comfort, and efficiency—as well as other values—conflict. Ask the students for examples, such as the conflict over the use of automobiles.

4. You may wish to begin—and extend—this focus on the media by analyzing a videotape of a popular television program, past or present. Through a stop-start chunking process, the instructor and the students do a freewrite analysis of what they see and hear in terms of values. Then instructor and students share what they wrote about the artifact:

Dominant American Values

1. Achievement and Success

In our competitive society, stress is placed on personal achievement. This is measured by accomplishments, such as economic ones. Success emphasizes rewards. Success is involved with activity; failure is often assigned to character defects. Success is often equated with bigness and newness.

2. Activity and Work

Americans also value busyness, speed, bustle, action. The frontier idea of work for survival is still with us, as is the Puritan ethic of work before play. Work becomes an end in itself. A person's worth is measured by his or her performance.

3. Moral Orientation

Americans think in terms of good and bad, right and wrong—not just in practical terms. Early Puritan ideas of working hard, leading an orderly life, having a reputation for integrity and fair dealing, avoiding reckless display, and carrying out one's purposes still hold weight.

4. Humanitarianism

Much emphasis is placed on disinterested concern, helpfulness, personal kindliness, aid and comfort, spontaneous aid in mass disasters, as well as on impersonal philanthropy. This emphasis is related to equalitarian democracy, but often it clashes with our value of rugged individualism.

5. Efficiency and Practicality

Germans refer to our "Fordismus" or belief in standardization, mass production, and streamlined industrialism. We like innovation, modernity, expediency, getting things done. We value technique and discipline in science. We enjoy short-range adjustments in immediate situations. Practicality again means active interest in workability.

6. Progress

Americans look forward more than backward. We resent the old-fashioned, the outmoded. We seek the best yet through change. Progress is often identified with the Darwinian idea of survival of the fittest and with the free enterprise system.

7. Material Comfort

Americans enjoy passive gratification—drink this, chew that, take a vacation. We enjoy happy endings in movies. We enjoy consumption, and our heroes before 1920 were more from social, commercial, and cultural worlds of production. After the 1920s the heroes came more from the leisure-time activities of sports and entertainment. Yet Americans also enjoy culture and engage in do-it-yourself hobbies and vacations.

8. Equality

Our history has stressed the equality of opportunity, especially economic opportunity. We feel guilt, shame, or ego deflation when inequalitarianism appears. While discrimination exists, much lip service is paid to formal rights, legal rights. Equality is not a pure concept but is largely two-sided: social rights and equality of opportunity.

9. Freedom

Americans also seek freedom from some restraint, having confidence in the individual. Freedom enters into free enterprise, progress, individual choice, and equality. It has not meant the absence of social control.

10. External Conformity

Americans also believe in adherence to group patterns, especially for success. Economic, political, and social dependence and interdependence call for some conformity. If all people are equal, each has a right to judge the other and regulate conduct to accepted standards.

11. Science

Americans have faith in science and its tools. Science is rational, functional, active. Science is morally neutral. It adds to our material comfort and progress.

12. Nationalism–Patriotism

Americans feel some sense of loyalty to their country, its national symbols, and its history. Foreigners observe how we value our flag and our national anthem, how we believe that America is the greatest country in the world.

13. Democracy

Americans have grown to accept majority rule, representative institutions, and to reject monarchies, aristocracies, and dictatorships. We accept law, equality, freedom.

14. Individual Personality

We protect our individualism by laws and by the belief in one's own worth.

15. Racism and Group Superiority

This is a deviant theme, not central, but still widespread. This value takes its form in racial, religious, ethnic, and sexual discrimination.

Adapted from Robin M. Williams, Jr., *American Society: A Sociological Interpretation*, 3rd ed. (New York: Alfred A. Knopf, 1960) 396–470.

Assignments—Values Transmission and Reinforcement

Handout 5

Directions

Below are two assignments for discovering how American values are transmitted and reinforced in contemporary society. Note the due dates.

Assignment 1

On the board is a list of the ten most popular television programs according to a recent poll. Because TV is one of the most popular of mass media, these programs should reveal dominant American values. Using the dominant values handout (Handout 4), take notes and analyze *one* of these programs. Write a short paper (minimum: one page) in which you discuss: (1) the plot of this program, (2) the dominant values you find in the program and in the sponsor's advertising. See how many values you can find, and be sure to give clear examples of each from the program. You should find at least eight values. Note: Study the handout of a model student artifact analysis (Handout 6). Announce the due date: _____ .

Assignment 2

Select one of the following suggestions for another method of discussing dominant American values. DUE: _____

1. Cut out ads from newspapers or magazines for each of the fifteen dominant American values. Identify each with a sentence or two of explanation.

2. Cut out a Sunday comic strip or any three newspaper cartoons. Then write a values analysis (at least one page) of the strip or the cartoons.

3. Observe any children's cartoon program on TV, such as one of the weekend series. Then write at least a one-page analysis of values being transmitted or reinforced.

4. Using a weekly newspaper or magazine TV guide, make an analysis (at least one page) of the types and frequency of programs on prime time (6:30 to 10:00 p.m.) on the three major networks. Do you feel that these types are in balance or are they too heavy on certain values?

5. Is American TV too violent? Select at least two popular programs that use violence in their plots. Do a "violence count"—the numbers

and types of violence responses—and draw your own conclusions. Note: Consider sharing your analysis with the class through videotape cuttings.

6. Are we really getting the "important" news? Observe and time a network (local or national) news program. Write an analysis (at least one page) on the values of the program; that is, the selection, the order of presentation, the time, the use of visuals or on-the-spot reporting, the time given to each item. Consider sharing your analysis with the class through videotape cuttings.

7. Why is Walt Disney so American? Study a Disney TV program or film. Or analyze one of his Dream Parks in California or Florida. Write at least one page on the things Disney values.

8. Take a poll of local students' Top Ten Heroes and Heroines. Work with a partner and make a video-poll and write at least a one-page analysis of your results.

9. Hero analysis: The faces of heroes and heroines are often on the covers of popular magazines. Read the cover story of a magazine (such as *Time, Newsweek,* or any teenage magazine) and then analyze (at least one page) the hero in terms of the dominant values.

10. Attend a local pep rally, sports event, concert, or meeting. Write at least one page about the values that cluster around this event. Suggestion: Pretend you are a foreign exchange student trying to make sense of a high school football game.

11. Examine an issue of your school newspaper, creative writing magazine, or yearbook. How do local journalists and editors choose and structure their news and school artifacts? Write at least a page.

12. Watch a TV special or telethon. Example: The Miss America Contest. Define the dominant values in one page or more.

13. You (and your partner or partners) may choose your own topic, your own method of presentation!

Handout 6

Model Student Artifact Analysis of a Popular TV Program

"M*A*S*H": Twelve Years of Success

What is it that keeps a television series on the top for twelve years? One way of answering that question is to analyze a thirty-minute segment of "M*A*S*H," a program so popular that its episodes are still rerun. The answer lies in the inherent American values, not just in the trends of the political, economic, and social climate.

The segment that I watched last Saturday on CBS concerned the American Korean War surgeons of the M*A*S*H unit who were working on the wounded for eighteen hours straight. The first value, achievement and success, was obvious. The surgeons were very successful and didn't lose a patient, even though they were under a great deal of pressure for a long time. The fact that they were in surgery for eighteen hours represents activity and work, as well as their skill with scientific training.

The fourth and fifth values represent moral orientation and humanitarianism. The doctors' profession and their Hippocratic oath demand a strong sense of morality and humanitarianism. Humanitarianism, for example, is revealed when a Puerto Rican is upset because the doctors had to shave off his mustache to perform surgery on his face, and Klinger makes a fake mustache out of his own hair for no other reason than to make the man feel better.

The doctors' hard work in surgery reveals efficiency and practicality. The patients come in and go out quickly, so no wounded person has to wait very long. The efficiency is a result of medical progress. The doctors in this episode had a baffling case where a man had not regained consciousness since arriving at the hospital. Because of his extensive medical knowledge, Colonel Potter was able to figure out the difficulty and cure the patient.

Equality and racism clash in this segment, too. An African American who is very important to his unit and helps rescue injured soldiers was teased by some white soldiers. Yet the way that Hawkeye reacts to them triggers a feeling of equality in the viewer.

The final value that I discovered in the segment was nationalism and patriotism. Major Hoolihan talks to a patient about how he got his wound. He says that when he and a North Korean looked directly at each other, both paused before they fired. She asks him if he killed the man. He enthusiastically answers yes, and she says, "Good for you!" This shows the kind of nationalism found in Americans during wartime.

The commercials drove home the familiar messages of fast food (efficient and practical), soft tissues (material comfort), soap ("You are not clean until you're zestfully clean"), and beer (patriotic red, white, and blue cans).

So there it is: TV as artifact, reflecting and molding American culture!

Lesson 5
Values and Consensus
Seeking: Fishbowling

Goal

This lesson has two interacting goals: reinforcing the previous lesson on heroes and heroines and beginning small group activity where consensus seeking will occur.

Materials

Handout 7: "Values and Consensus Seeking." The sample following this lesson has a 1960s decade focus, as well as a concern for more recent values. You can alter the handout by using the latest polls on any topic. These often appear around the end of the year in newspapers and magazines, such as *Good Housekeeping* (in January), that conduct their own popularity polls, which tend to reflect the values of their readership. The *Gallup Poll Monthly* also publishes national polls.

Procedure

1. Review the previous discussion of heroes as a cultural phenomenon. Note that while not everyone agrees on heroes and heroines, there is usually a national consensus about those at the top, such as the President.

2. Ask for volunteers or pick six to eight students, the usual size of a small group, for consensus seeking. Then ask them to leave the room for a few minutes.

3. While this group is outside, distribute Handout 7, "Values and Consensus Seeking." Review the directions: (a) The results are not in order, but are scrambled. (b) The small group will put the poll in order as they see it. (c) Observers will evaluate the success of the group in reaching its goal.

4. Ask or pick four volunteers to take notes and be ready to evaluate the success of the small group in reaching its goal on each of the four points listed at the bottom of the handout.

5. Ask the small group to return and form a circle inside the class—as if they were in a fishbowl. Distribute the handout to the group,

noting the poll and the directions at the top. Tell them that they have twenty minutes to unscramble a scrambled poll, ranking the names or items, from 1 to 10, in the order that they feel was the final result. The group is to achieve this goal by consensus, through any method they wish.

6. The discussion will reveal students' values, background information, and powers of analysis and persuasion, as well as their use of dominant values. It will reveal the problems and successes of group interaction, especially in a group that has no appointed chair or recorder.

7. At the end of about fifteen minutes, ask a member of the group to write the final list on the board. Then ask each of the four observers to describe the small group in terms of one of the four points: group participation, influence, group atmosphere, and methods of consensus. The observers' evaluations will be useful to members of the group, as well as to the class, in preparation for small groups later.

8. The instructor writes the actual results on the board. The class discusses the two polls, their reaction to differences among the small-group guesses, and the values implied in the rankings.

9. The instructor summarizes the reactions and stresses the successes of this first small group. Students should be reminded that in the future the small groups will have leaders, recorders, observers-evaluators—and plenty of time to prepare for specific topics, such as the analysis of decade artifacts.

Additional Suggestions and Alternatives

1. Reveal the 1980 results of the teenage poll, noting the major shifts in twenty years. How do the students account for these shifts? Ask the students to compare these polls with their present influences. Take a straw poll on this topic in class.

2. A challenging alternative that involves knowledge of the 1960s is a Gallup Poll on "Most Admired Man of 1966" and "Most Admired Woman of 1965." The poll asked, "What man/woman that you have heard or read about, living today in any part of the world, do you admire the most?"

Correct Answers

Most Admired Man, 1966: (1) Lyndon Johnson, (2) Dwight Eisenhower, (3) Robert Kennedy, (4) Billy Graham, (5) Pope Paul VI, (6) Martin Luther King, (7) Richard Nixon, (8) Hubert Humphrey, (9) Barry Goldwater, (10) Harry Truman.

Most Admired Woman, 1965: (1) Mrs. John Kennedy, (2) Mrs. Lyndon Johnson, (3) Queen Elizabeth II, (4) Margaret Chase Smith, (5) Clare Boothe Luce, (6) Helen Keller, (7) Mrs. Dwight Eisenhower, (8) Pearl Buck, (9) Mme. Chiang Kai-shek, (10) Marian Anderson.

Correct Answers to Handout 7

1960	1980
1. Mother, father	1. Friends, peers
2. Teachers	2. Mother, father
3. Friends, peers	3. Television, radio, records, cinema
4. Ministers, priests, rabbis	4. Teachers
5. Youth club leaders, counselors, advisers, scoutmasters, coaches, librarians	5. Popular heroes, idols in sports, music
6. Popular heroes, idols in sports, music	6. Ministers, priests, rabbis
7. Grandparents, uncles, aunts	7. Newspapers, magazines
8. Television, radio, records, cinema	8. Advertising
9. Newspapers, magazines	9. Youth club leaders, counselors, advisers, scoutmasters, coaches, librarians
10. Advertising	10. Grandparents, uncles, aunts

Values and Consensus Seeking

Handout
7

Every year national polls seek to find American attitudes about everything from favorite sports to the most admired men and women in the world. Below are two scrambled lists of the results for such a poll.

Your small group will be given about fifteen (15) minutes to arrive at consensus on what you believe was the national response to the same question that was asked of teenagers in either 1960 or 1980.

In other words, put in order what you believe to be the result of the poll in that year. Remember, the top choice is 1 and the lowest is 10.

"What are the major influences in your life?"*

1. Television, radio, records, cinema
2. Ministers, priests, rabbis
3. Friends, peers
4. Advertising
5. Grandparents, uncles, aunts
6. Teachers
7. Popular heroes, idols in sports, music
8. Mother, father
9. Newspapers, magazines
10. Youth club leaders, counselors, advisers, scoutmasters, coaches, librarians

* "How Teenagers Rate Major Influences on Their Lives," *Des Moines Register*, November 5, 1981. Based on research of the Junior Achievement/Robert Johnson opinion poll of 2,200 teenagers across the country.

Specific Instructions:

1. Avoid arguing. Approach the task on the basis of logic.

2. Don't change your mind to avoid conflict. Modify your position so that it allows you to support logical solutions or at least partial agreement.

3. Avoid conflict-reducing techniques such as a majority vote.

4. Avoid pressuring and bringing into line individuals to reduce your own feelings of tension.

5. View differences of opinion as helpful.

The Observers: Your job is to observe the group operation, the way they handle a problem in seeking consensus. Consider the following points:

1. *Participation:* Did everyone participate? Who participated the most? Did anyone assume leadership? Did someone become a recorder or secretary? Did anyone dominate the discussion? Did they leave the subject?

2. *Influence:* In what ways did the group members influence each other—facts, logic, argument, raising their voice, pressuring? Did they listen to each other? Did they respond to each other? Did some give in to be pleasant?

3. *Group atmosphere:* Were the members cooperative and pleasant? Were they intense? Did anything prevent consensus?

4. *Methods of consensus:* How did they try to achieve consensus? Did they vote on each point or begin with number 1 or number 10? Did they use some method of solving serious disagreements? In what ways did they modify their positions?

Small-group work is important in American Humanities!

Lesson 6
Culture Shock

Goal

Understanding the values of people from different cultures and how they can experience culture shock.

Materials

Invite one or more foreign students or visitors to the class. If none are available, find people who have recently traveled to another country. Or invite multicultural students from your own school.

Assignment

1. Remind the students of the due date for the first assignment on the value study sheet (Handout 5).

2. Tell the students to begin the second assignment on Handout 5. Refer to the sheet and the variety of choices. Announce the due date:

_____ .

Procedure

1. After announcing the assignment, introduce the visitor who has lived in or visited another culture. Ask the visitor or the class to give a few facts about the culture. Use a map.

2. Remind the students that it is often difficult to live in another culture; one can experience culture shock when one encounters different values. Remind them of how difficult it might be if they were sent as exchange students for one year to live in that culture and go to school there. Outsiders are often good observers of things people in a culture take for granted and no longer notice. The object of the lesson is to learn about each other, not to prove which culture is better.

3. The discussion may begin with the visitor inviting questions or telling about his or her culture, or the instructor can lead with an American Humanities question such as the following: What differences exist between your culture and American cultures and subcultures? During the discussion, the instructor should seek answers to other cultural questions: (a) How did you learn about American society? (b) Did

America turn out to be different from what you expected? (c) Who are the heroes of your culture? (d) What concrete word or object symbolizes your culture, as well as America's? (e) What do you like or dislike about America?

4. About five or ten minutes before the period ends, thank the visitor for coming. After the visitor leaves, invite the students to respond to the visitor's values and observations.

Alternatives and Suggestions

1. Begin the individual folder system. Distribute folders stapled with the "Folder Record—First Period Evaluations by Instructor and Observers." (See Handout 19 after Lesson 40.) Ask the students to write their name and period on the front. Review the scope of the first grading period. Tell the students where these folders will be located in the classroom. The folder system reviews the students' total achievement.

2. Open class discussion by having all students discuss their travels to other cultures *outside* or *inside* the United States—to an American small town or a large city, to a new school or neighborhood where old values are challenged. The instructor should share personal experience as well or introduce cultural topics that will interest students. Example: body language. Various cultures have different attitudes about touching, holding hands, crossing legs, kissing, even the physical distance between people while they are eating or talking.

3. Encourage visitors to bring some of their own cultural artifacts that can be compared with our artifacts—and lead our study toward the next assignment.

Lesson 7
Individual Values
Clarification

Goal

Clarifying and contrasting individual values and dominant American values.

Materials

A dollar bill (for purposes of the assignment for Lessons 8 and 9).

Assignment

Describe Artifact Days, Lessons 8 and 9, during which the students should bring one American object-artifact that reveals American values and be ready to speak about it. They are to look closely at the artifact, as if it were found by anthropologists. See how many of the fifteen dominant values (Handout 4) are related to the artifact. Use the dollar bill as a model: (1) the product of science and technology; (2) a practical, billfold-sized instrument for getting things done; (3) a picture of a hero, a symbol of our first (successful) president (patriotism and nationalism); (4) progress from the old barter system; (5) moral orientation, "In God We Trust."

Procedure

1. Announce the Artifact Days assignment. Use the dollar bill example. Note: You may choose to announce this assignment as a short speech to be given in front of the class with open discussion or as a presentation to a small group.

2. Note that future archaeologists may find some of the artifacts and use them to determine the nature of American civilization. Ask the students what archaeologists usually find. Discuss time capsules.

3. This lesson attempts to clarify individual student values. Ask for or pick at least three volunteers. Write their names on the board, draw vertical lines to separate each name.

4. Announce that each student has just won a huge cash prize, say $2,000,000, by winning a state or national contest or lottery.

5. Steps for values clarification (ask each student the same question before moving on to the next):

    a. Ask the students to describe what they will do *first* with the money, and place their answers beneath their names.

    b. Ask them other key questions and write their responses: Will they quit school? Go on to higher education? Where will they live? Will they get married and have children? Will they have a job?

    c. If they have invested or saved their money, what will they do next?

6. Challenge the students' values: Why should they go to school or work if they have all this money? It could be invested for an excellent annual income.

7. Call on the class to identify which of the fifteen dominant values seem to be most important for each student and all students. Write those on the board as well.

8. Finally, ask the students to reflect on lottery and prize winners. Why do people enter such contests? Who wins, who loses?

Lessons 8–9
Everyday Objects
as Artifacts

Goal

Understanding everyday objects as artifacts of modern American culture representing various values.

Materials

Each student should bring one artifact to class.

Procedure

1. Remind the students of the due date for the second values assignment (Handout 5). Note: You also may wish to have students present these assignments during Lesson 10.

2. Review the previous concepts of culture, values, and artifacts.

3. Ask the students to describe their objects and to define them in terms of American values.

4. Encourage the class to respond to each artifact, expanding on their experiences with the artifact. These anecdotal discussions can be very useful and hold the interest of the class. The instructor should enter into the discussion and bring an artifact, too.

5. When everyone is finished during the ninth lesson, ask the students to name artifacts that also might have been discussed.

Alternative and Additional Suggestions

1. Instead of more formal speeches that take two days, the class can be divided into small groups for a one-day lesson. Procedure:

    a. Each student shows the group the artifact but does no analysis.

    b. All group members do a freewrite entry in their journals about the artifact.

    c. Then the student who has shown the artifact calls on one or more group members to read their entries.

    d. Finally, the student responds to their entries and completes his or her analysis.

   e. When the group is finished, the members pick one student to represent their group and describe his or her artifact to the class.

2. If the small-group procedure is used for day 8, then day 9 may be used for additional artifact analysis. Suggestions:

   a. A freewrite and discussion on a topic: "The Perfect Time Capsule for Our School (or for Teenage Culture or for Our Country)."

   b. A reading of and response to *The Weans*, by Robert Nathan; to "History Lesson," by Arthur C. Clarke, found in *Across the Stars*; to *Motel of Mysteries*, by David Macaulay.

Lesson 10
The Idea of Culture:
Conclusion

Goal

Providing flexible choices to review and reinforce the concepts of the first ten lessons, "The Idea of Culture."

Materials

Materials for the last lesson in this section will follow the choices already determined by the previous lessons.

Procedure

1. During the first half of the period, complete the previous study, reinforce what students have learned, or finish instruction. Choices:

   a. Have individual students or small groups present their second values assignments from Handout 5.

   b. Use the media to review values or the concept of humanities. Suggestion: See the Bibliography.

   c. Use cultural theories with selected works:
      - How American sex roles began to blend by the 1960s. Use Charles Winick's book, *The New People.*
      - Ask students to plan a summer trip in Japan. Use Gary Katzenstein's *Funny Business: An Outsider's Year in Japan.*
      - Ask the students to do a class analysis of their living room— "The Living Room Scale" in Paul Fussell's *Class.*
      - Ask the male students to describe the "rites of passage" for becoming a man in America. Use Ray Raphael's *The Men from the Boys,* especially chapter 9, "Zero-Sum Contests," in terms of the meaning of sports.

2. The second half of the class period should be a freewrite that will be handed in and included in the student folders: "What Did I Learn During This First Section?"

3. Now the students are ready to use the ideas and tools of these lessons in the weeks ahead when they examine an American decade. They will be studying a recent historical period that has shaped many of the values of today.

Lessons 11–26
The Historical Period: 1960s

Active exchange with other students and the teacher is crucial for making learning an integral part of the student's experience. The subject matter is important not only for its own sake, but also as a way of developing transferable abilities in writing, reading, and thinking.

The English Coalition: Democracy through Language (85)

Lesson 11
Orientation to a Decade

Goal

Beginning the orientation to the 1960s. Beginning research and involvement with the people of the decade.

Materials

Handout 8: "Names and Terms of the Decade: 1960s."

Assignment

The students are to write a one-line explanation of each term on a separate sheet of paper. They may work together in pairs, using the materials of the classroom, the school, and the community. Encourage them to interview their family members and neighbors.

Procedure

1. Review the first ten lessons, stressing methods that will be used in the decade study, especially artifact analysis.

2. Using the chalkboard, make three columns:

    1945–60   **1960–70**   **1970–80**

    Ask the students to volunteer what they know or think they know about these time periods. Ask for categories: presidents, historical events, sports, books, films, music, art, architecture, dances, fads, inventions. Clarify material that is or is not in the 1960s. Also offer suggestions, but avoid generalizations that can bias the students throughout the course.

3. Distribute copies of the names and terms handout. Clarify the assignment and due date: _____ .

4. To initiate the research, explain any five terms that the students feel they do not know. Be prepared to expand on one term to stimulate interest in the material. Some students may know many of the terms, and you should encourage their sharing their information. (Many of the terms can be found in the history readings listed in the Bibliography and in Lesson 12.)

5. Remind the students that the first days of the history section will involve building their history background through research, documentary films, small groups and committees, oral history, and family history.

Additional Suggestions

1. To whet curiosity and relate to the lesson of Artifact Days, the instructor displays or initiates a lesson with a high school artifact of the 1960s, such as clothing, a yearbook, newspaper, school student handbook, record cover, photograph.

2. Develop a classroom library of reference books and materials, especially ones that have photographs. Encourage the students to examine these books for term research.

Names and Terms of the Decade: 1960s

Handout

8

DUE: _____

Directions: Identify each term in one good sentence:

1. JFK
2. freedom riders
3. "We Shall Overcome"
4. hippies
5. Lee Harvey Oswald
6. USS *Pueblo*
7. "Laugh-In"
8. Eugene McCarthy
9. SDS
10. *Soul on Ice*
11. "The Eagle Has Landed"
12. Twiggy
13. Joan Baez
14. *In Cold Blood*
15. honkies
16. Charlie Brown
17. Bob Dylan
18. The Beatles
19. groovy
20. LSD
21. Spiro Agnew
22. Woodstock Festival
23. *Hair*
24. Malcolm X
25. Timothy Leary
26. SNCC
27. John Updike
28. Kate Millett
29. Cuban Missile Crisis
30. Andy Warhol
31. Pope John XXIII
32. Angela Davis
33. Joe Namath
34. *The Sound of Music*
35. Black Power
36. Jerry Rubin
37. George Wallace
38. Walter Cronkite
39. Robert Kennedy
40. Edward Albee
41. Ho Chi Minh Trail
42. "Gunsmoke"
43. Marshall McLuhan
44. Norman Mailer
45. James Earl Ray
46. *Easy Rider*
47. Martin Luther King, Jr.
48. "The Beverly Hillbillies"
49. Mario Savio
50. The Twist
51. commune
52. Jimi Hendrix
53. Maharishi
54. Sirhan Sirhan
55. miniskirts
56. Warren Report
57. funky
58. Tet Offensive
59. *Doctor Zhivago*
60. Watts
61. Leroi Jones
62. Dick Gregory

63. Raquel Welch
64. Tiny Tim
65. *Valley of the Dolls*
66. pigs
67. moratorium
68. doves and hawks
69. *Go Tell It on the Mountain*
70. Johnny Carson
71. James Bond (007)
72. Richard Daley
73. Rachel Carson
74. Dr. Benjamin Spock
75. Silent Majority
76. Black Panthers
77. *Hello Dolly!*
78. Lester Maddox
79. The Boston Strangler
80. Charles Manson
81. "Blowin' in the Wind"
82. Fidel Castro
83. Sylvia Plath
84. ecology
85. *Who's Afraid of Virginia Woolf?*
86. My Lai
87. geodesic dome
88. Vince Lombardi
89. Arnold Palmer
90. John Glenn
91. Cassius Clay/Muhammad Ali
92. The Rolling Stones
93. Lawrence Ferlinghetti
94. Robert Rauschenberg
95. Claes Oldenburg
96. Mickey Mantle
97. DMZ
98. Betty Friedan
99. Roy Lichtenstein
100. Chappaquiddick

Lessons 12–14
History of the Decade

Goal

Reinforcement of student research on terms. Orientation to the historical period through audiovisual materials.

Materials

1. Handout 1: "American Humanities: Tentative Schedule for the 1960s." Note the word *tentative*, because both teacher and students may decide to change the order and materials of the schedule. The schedule is to remain flexible to meet the needs of the class, as well as the alterations of a continually changing all-school environment.

2. Assigned reading for small-group discussions. Suggestions:

   a. *Waking from the Dream: America in the Sixties*, by Toby Goldstein. This is a short, highly readable book (in paperback) for high school students. It can be read in its entirety for small-group discussion.

   b. *Coming Apart*, by William L. O'Neill. This is a long, more challenging but also highly readable book (paperback) for college prep students. Certainly the chapter on "Counterculture" should be considered for the reading assignment.

   c. Some teachers may wish to combine sections from these two books.

3. Artifacts of the decade to initiate the lesson, or the Time-Life book, *This Fabulous Century, 1960–1970*, volume 7.

4. Audiovisual materials. Suggestions: (a) an overall decade film; (b) a sequence of films about the three presidents—Kennedy, Johnson, Nixon; (c) a Vietnam film. (Note: films on these topics also can reinforce other sections of the course.) See Bibliography.

Assignments

1. The students should continue working together on the names and terms sheet (Handout 8).

2. The students should begin reading the pages determined by the instructor.

Procedure

1. The lesson could begin with the use of an artifact to remind the students of the 1960s. Ask them if they have any 1960s artifacts in their homes. Later, an artifact committee will be making a presentation.

2. Distribute Handout 1. Note the scope of the course, as well as the assignments in the history section, especially the reading requirement for small groups.

3. Distribute the history reading, noting that this material will help them with their terms, too.

4. Small-group procedures will be discussed later, but students should be told that they will be asked to take notes on their reading, notes on such questions as "What are the major characteristics of the 1960s?" and "What important things were happening that may have a bearing on today?"

5. Days 12 and 14 should be used for reading and research, partners sharing their answers, and audiovisual reinforcement.

Additional Suggestions

Be sure that the students have time to discuss the films. What terms did they find in each film? What questions do they have about content? You may wish to stop-start segments of the film to avoid passive film watching. This chunking technique can be accompanied by journal freewrites and sharing.

Lesson 15
History: Small-Group Activities

Goal

Preparation for small-group discussion. Establishing activity committees, which will work on reinforcement tasks when not in small-group discussions.

Materials

Handout 9: "Small-Group Discussion Procedures."

Assignment

1. Announce the activity committees first. Take volunteers for the Handbook Committee, the Bulletin Board Committee, the Artifacts Committee, and the Media Committee.

2. Then organize the History Small Groups, trying to keep the students on the same activity committees together, since they must work as units on their topic when their History Small Group is not meeting.

Procedure

1. Students should be reminded of the due date for the names and terms assignment (Handout 8), preferably by Lesson 16.

2. Before discussing small-group procedures, stress that activity committees will function when the students are not in small-group sessions. Refer to the tentative schedule (Handout 1). These activities will reinforce what the students are reading and will be useful later in oral history sessions and preparation for projects.

3. Activity Committees:

    a. *Committee 1: The Handbook Committee.* This committee will make a class handbook, with each student writing (typing or word processing) a one-page "Story of the Year" or a "Major Events of the Year" for each year of the 1960s. This committee can consist of ten to twenty students. (See examples and format that follow this lesson.) If the class is very large, or if the instructor wishes to drop committees 2, 3, or 4, the handbook could be extended with an introduction, a decade slang dictionary, articles of famous personalities (man/woman of the year/decade), a page on fads. Be sure to appoint a student to make the cover for the handbook.

b. *Committee 2: The Bulletin Board Committee.* This group of three to five students should be responsible for making a class bulletin board that conveys their concept of the decade. It is interesting to see how this concept holds up during the course.

c. *Committee 3: The Artifacts Committee.* This committee of three to eight students should be responsible for an artifact presentation day (or part of a period). They must gather materials. A fashion show, a skit built around an idea, or an "antique show" make excellent programs.

d. *Committee 4: The Media Committee.* Members of this committee will work closely together making a media production. Suggestions: a radio or TV newscast based on 1960s artifacts such as local newspapers; a parody of a popular TV program; a serious or amusing enactment of a 1960s event, such as "Life Among the Hippies" or "A Day at Woodstock."

Note: Each activity committee should choose a chair who will delegate responsibilities, a secretary who will record the members' names and responsibilities, and an observer who, along with the secretary, will report to the instructor for evaluation.

4. History Small Groups:

a. Distribute the handout on small-group procedures (Handout 9). During Lesson 18, these procedures will be reviewed and time will be given for reading and for meetings of activity committees.

b. Because students will be in both activity committees and history small groups, try to keep activity committee members in the same history group. This ensures a smoother functioning of both groups.

Small-Group Discussion Procedures

Name, Period: _____

Subject for Discussion: _____

Due Date: _____

Members of the Group:

1.   6.

2.   7.

3.   8.

4.   9.

5   10.

Chair:

Secretary-Recorder:

Observer:

Procedure: Consensus Seeking

The small groups will meet after you have done the readings and taken notes on content and such questions as "What are the major characteristics of this period?"

    The group will select a chair, a secretary-recorder, and an observer. The chair will see that individual members contribute from their notes at least one of their own ten characteristics of the period. Then the small group must arrive at ten consensus characteristics. The secretary-recorder will record these statements and give them to the instructor at the end of the period. The observers will make oral evaluations at the end of the period and collect the notes and books.

    Points for the observers to consider:

1. *Participation:* Did everyone participate? Did everyone add one characteristic to the list? Did all students carry out their roles?

2. *Preparation:* Was everyone prepared? Did each student use notes and refer to the reading? Did any members refer directly to the reading? Did they cite or read anything?

3. *American Humanities method:* Did the group reach its goal? Were their consensus statements, individually and as a group, objective, analytical, and useful for later consideration? Did the students try to answer any "whys"? Were they interested in values?

4. *Atmosphere:* Was the group cooperative and friendly in the spirit of consensus?

Note: Be sure to bring your books and notes to the small group.

Evaluation of Small Groups

Whether the instructor uses the *H, S, U* or traditional grading system, students need to be evaluated, especially to reward them for their individual and group preparation and efforts. The suggested "Evaluation Vehicle" that follows is a kind of verbal basketball "shot-chart" where the total achievement of each student is noted, especially in terms of preparation, participation, and individual and group effort. The roles of chair, secretary-recorder, and observer should rotate during the course. Note: The group receives a grade, too—and this is averaged into individual evaluations. These evaluations should be placed in the students' folders.

Sample Evaluation Vehicle for History Small Groups

Handout

Name, Period: _____

Small Group: History Consensus

1. Quality of Notes, Use of Notes: _____

2. Participation, Major Contributions: _____
   a. Individual
   b. Chair
   c. Secretary-Recorder
   d. Observer

3. Efforts at Consensus: _____

4. Group Evaluation: _____

Folder Grade: _____

Comments:

Center for Teaching
The Westminster Schools

George W. Woodruff Library
The Westminster Schools

Sample Major Events of the Year 1968 from a Class Handbook

1968

Politics

1. In a dramatic television appearance on March 31, President Johnson announced that he would not seek re-election.
2. On June 26, Robert Kennedy died from assassination in Los Angeles.
3. On August 8, in Miami, Richard Nixon easily defeated Governor Reagan of California and Governor Rockefeller of New York for the Republican nomination for the presidency.

Statistics

1. During 1968, 1,444,780 mobile homes were owned by Americans.
2. There were a total of 5,261,206 arrests of all ages in the United States.
3. Unemployment of blue collar workers varied between 3.7 and 4.5 million.

Art, Literature, and Music

1. *The Money Game* was a best-selling non-fiction novel.
2. On August 13, Rene d'Haroncourt, a leading figure in the art world and former director of the Museum of Modern Art in New York, died at age 67.
3. "Hey, Jude," by the Beatles, hit the top singles chart on September 28.

Science and Technology

1. Philip Blaiberg, the longest surviving heart transplant patient, received his new heart on January 2 in an operation performed by Dr. Christiaan Barnard.
2. On December 24, the Apollo VIII crew saw the far side of the moon.
3. During July of 1968, two oil companies exploring the Arctic coast of Alaska discovered the largest oil field in the Western Hemisphere.

Sports

1. On January 1, Southern California defeated Indiana, 14–3, in the Rose Bowl, thanks to the powerful running back O. J. Simpson.
2. On February 10, figure skater Peggy Fleming won the Olympic gold medal for ice skating.

3. On September 19, pitcher Denny McLain was the first 31-game winner since 1931.

Movies

1. *The Graduate* was the year's most popular film.
2. On June 12, *Rosemary's Baby,* starring Mia Farrow, was released.
3. On November 13, *Yellow Submarine* premiered, music by the Beatles.

Miscellaneous

1. *The Pueblo,* a U.S. navy ship, was captured by the North Korean patrol boats and taken into port.
2. On April 11, the 1968 Civil Rights Act was signed by President Johnson.
3. Helen Keller died at the age of 87, a famous American who had been deaf, dumb, and blind since infancy.

Sample Story: 1961 from a Class Handbook

The Sky Is No Longer the Limit

The nation watched. A figure resembling a creature from outer-space entered the Redstone rocket. However, he was not from outer-space; he was preparing to enter it. The year was 1961. The man in the silver space suit was Alan B. Shepard.

A tremendous flame shot out, scorching the pad, as the rocket rose. In lift-off, Shepard radioed a message: "Roger . . . lift-off . . . the clock is started." Yes, the clock had started; the space race was on.

The US vs Russia race was a real challenge for our country.

Though Shepard had been the first American in space, it was a Russian, Yuri Gagarin, who had preceded him by three weeks. The Russian challenge was especially troubling since we had live television coverage of our space flights while the Soviets announced Gagarin's flight only after his successful landing.

President John Kennedy reminded Americans of the challenges and the rewards. He said, "The opening vistas of space promise high costs and hardships, as well as high reward." Congress supported the President's space program by allocating $1.1 billion for it in 1961.

The hardships to which President Kennedy referred would become evident during the flight of Virgil "Gus" Grissom on July 21. Using a more advanced capsule, Grissom followed a flight plan identical to that of Shepard's. The capsule landed safely in the ocean, 302 miles from Cape Canaveral.

While the astronaut waited quietly inside the capsule for the helicopter, the hatch blew open, triggered by the waves. Grissom scrambled through the hatch and into the sea. Even without a helmet, the suit should have floated, but Grissom had not closed an intake port of his suit. Slowly, he began to sink. The helicopter arrived just in the nick of time. Filled with water, the five ton capsule had to be abandoned.

It was 1961—the first journeys outside the earth's atmosphere. And our pace did not slacken. Each space flight improved upon the technology of the previous one. We looked to new horizons: a successful orbit around the earth, a landing on the moon—and beyond. The year 1961 began a decade of extraordinary progress in space exploration into a new frontier.

Lesson 16
History: Small-Group Activities

Goal

Preparation for small-group discussions. Preparation for activity committees.

Materials

1. Handout 9: "Small-Group Discussion Procedures."

2. Optional: sample (major events and story of the year) from class handbooks; small-group evaluation forms (texts at end of Lesson 15).

Procedure

1. Remind students about the activity committees. Make sure that everyone is on a committee. If the Handbook Committee is formed, make sure that all of the years of the era are taken. Distribute or post examples of the handbook entries. Photocopies can be made of students' work for a class handbook.

2. Distribute the handout on small-group procedures. Review:

   a. Small groups will consist of five to ten students. There will be four groups, which correspond to the activity committees.

   b. The small group will decide the lesson day on which they wish to meet. (Or the instructor may prefer that the groups with faster readers go first.) The time also depends on the nature of their activity responsibilities; for example, the TV group may need to come last because of editing. Due dates for both of the assignments should be clarified.

   c. Each group will select a chair, a secretary-recorder, and an observer on the day of the discussion. The instructor will also be an observer. Note: The instructor may prefer to hold off student observers until the second small-group experience, because students will be more familiar with the expectations and procedures by then.

   d. Small groups must come prepared for consensus. Their goal is to arrive at ten consensus statements about the decade. Their notes should reflect not only content, but also their own suggestions for ten characteristics of the decade. The instructor may wish to use an example to clarify a "characteristic" versus just facts. (See "Sample History Consensus" below.)

e. The chair will ask each member to contribute at least one characteristic. The secretary-recorder will record the final ten statements agreed upon by the group and give them to the instructor. Near the end of the period, the instructor and observer will evaluate the group. Notes and books will be collected. (See Handout 9 on procedures.)

3. The instructor will compile all of the groups' ten consensus statements for Lesson 21, during which a class consensus will be taken.

4. The remaining time should be spent on reading or activity committee meetings. Students should be reminded that when they are not in small-group discussions, their activity committees can meet—or they can prepare for their small groups.

Sample History Consensus by a High School Class

The 1960s is best characterized as a time when . . .

1. All through the decade there was increasing political assassination, including JFK in 1963, Malcolm X in 1965, RFK and Martin Luther King in 1968, which affected the political mood of the nation.

2. The civil rights movement progressively gained support, becoming a major social, political, economic, and moral issue which led to riots, protests, rallies, sit-ins, freedom marches, and laws—such as the Civil Rights Act of 1964.

3. The women's movement was revitalized, starting with JFK's 1961 Committee to Investigate Women's Status, and led to many national organizations, such as NOW.

4. The 1960s foreign policy was a reaction to the Cold War when the United States was suspicious of Russia; this fear resulted in the Cuban Missile Crisis, the Bay of Pigs, and escalation of our involvement in the space race and the Vietnam War.

5. The nation was divided by an ideological struggle between the values and mores of the Establishment and figures of authority and the disillusioned, especially the youth.

6. The arts were dominated by a sexual revolution: changes in obscenity laws in literature, experimentation in the theater, and dramatically new lyrics in 1960s songs—all parts of the growing social and political changes in American life.

7. It was an age of new freedom, especially in the media and in exterior appearance—hair style and clothing.

8. With the 1960s came the counter-culture—a generation gap, whose anti-establishment attitudes were to be seen in such things as music and drugs.

9. Sports became more popular and organized—more money, more TV, big drawing cards from the Green Bay Packers to Arnold Palmer.

10. Problems in the cities became more and more serious—rising crime, strikes by city employees, a breakdown of services.

Lessons 17–20
History: Consensus Seeking

Goal

Consensus seeking by small groups on the history of the decade. Meetings of the activity committees or preparation for small groups.

Materials

1. History books and notes for small-group discussions.

2. Extra small-group discussion handouts on procedures (Handout 9).

3. Materials that activity committees might need, for example, bulletin board supplies, scissors, and staplers.

4. Optional: "Sample Evaluation Vehicle for History Small Groups."

Procedure

1. The instructor should remind the students of their small-group and activity committee responsibilities.

2. When the students are not in small-group discussion, they should remain in the classroom, go to the school library or resource center, or have open privileges for research, reading, or meetings. The values of freedom and group responsibility are essential to American Humanities. During this first experience, the instructor should reinforce the successes of each day and swiftly respond to individuals who violate those values. The success of the class depends on responsibility.

3. The small groups should meet, select a chair, a secretary-recorder, a student observer (optional). See also "Sample Evaluation Vehicle."

4. The instructor may wish to suggest a procedure. Example: The chair asks each student to suggest a different characteristic. The secretary records them. Then the chair asks the group to review each suggestion, deciding which are acceptable to the group, which need rewording or combining. This will lead to a final ten, as the students weigh characteristics and wording.

5. If student observers are chosen by the instructor, they should meet with the instructor and review the evaluation form or standards. The form may also be posted on the bulletin board for all students. Evaluation

of the student observers should include collecting their notes, observing their evaluations, and a brief follow-up conference.

6. At the end of the session, the instructor (and student observer, if used) should make final evaluative comments, as well as collect notes and books.

Lesson 21
History: Consensus Seeking

Goal

Class consensus on characteristics of the period, developed in small groups. Introduction to the concepts of oral history, genealogy, date research.

Materials

1. A composite of all the small-group consensus statements.

2. Sample genealogy charts, date research papers, a decade newspaper or magazine, oral history tapes. Audio-video tapes and players. The instructor could make an oral history sample or family chart before the course is taught—or during Lesson 22.

3. Handout 10: "Oral History, Date Research, Genealogy."

Assignments

1. Remind the students of due dates for activity committee reports and presentations, especially for the class handbook.

2. Students should volunteer for oral history, genealogy, and date research assignments. Encourage partners for oral history. Note the due dates by referring to the tentative schedule (Handout 1).

Procedure

1. The handbook should be ready for use in oral history.

2. Summarize the conclusions of small-group discussions.

3. Give every student a copy of the composite consensus statement. Ask the students to narrow the list to a final ten by circling their choices. No order of importance is necessary. Then ask them to list the number of circled statements at the bottom of the page. The instructor should collect the sheets, compile the class consensus, and later give copies to the students. (See Lesson 23.)

4. Discuss the next method of testing history, of discovering history, especially one's own history. Distribute Handout 10, refer to the assignment, announce due dates.

5. Use tapes, charts, and student papers. (See the sample papers that follow this lesson.)

a. *Oral history:* Discuss the problems of interviewing, of how to get people to remember (by using the handbook or by reviewing the decade) before turning on the tape player or video recorder. Encourage the interviewees to focus on memorable events, not generalities—focus on a key topic such as school or on a key event such as the day Kennedy was shot, their first car, high school graduation, a concert or protest. If you have sample tapes, share them in terms of their strengths and weaknesses: the sound quality, the information, whether the interview confirms or denies the class history consensus.

Encourage the students to interview relatives and neighbors, to send blank tapes and questions to relatives who live far away. Encourage partners to tape or videotape their interviews. This assignment could lead to a project, such as an in-depth study of a 1960s marriage or a comparison of teenage life in the 1960s versus today.

Students should be ready to discuss how their cuttings confirm or deny what the class has learned about the 1960s. They may refer to their papers.

b. *Genealogy:* Discuss how information can be gathered—through memory, family bibles and artifacts, newspaper clippings, photograph albums, birth and death certificates, marriage licenses. Students may write or call relatives or send them audiotapes, do research in local and county libraries or genealogical libraries. As the students build their "pedigree charts," they will find some information to be questionable, but all that is part of the excitement of primary research. Encourage them to gather family stories and mythologies as they share their "roots" with the class.

When the students present their charts, they should be ready to discuss what their research suggests about the 1960s.

c. *Date research:* Discuss how to find 1960s newspapers or magazines. Remind the students that relatives and neighbors often save old newspapers and magazines or that back issues can be found in community libraries, often on microfilm, and may be photocopied.

Encourage the students to focus on a date that interests them, such as a major historical event, an important day for their family, the day they were born versus that day in the 1960s. Encourage them to study the specific and the general— a key or feature story, topics that interest them, organization of the artifact, the advertising. They should reflect on the similarities and differences between these artifacts and the newspapers and magazines today. The students may refer to their papers in the presentation.

Additional and Alternative Suggestions

1. During this lesson or on the following four days, the instructor or the students could invite history teachers, senior citizens, members of local historical societies, and other resource persons to interact with the students. These interviews could be audiotaped or videotaped as well. It is important that community members of different ages and backgrounds reflect on this complex period, people who were teenagers, college students, parents, minorities, Vietnam soldiers.

2. You may wish to investigate conference telephone calls with resource persons inside and outside the community. This is especially useful for talking with invalids and older citizens, busy community people who can spare fifteen minutes during their work, experts on the decade. Suggestion: a local disc jockey who can both talk and play recordings of the 1960s over the phone or radio.

3. Model student oral history and date research papers may be distributed or posted on the bulletin board during this lesson or later.

4. You should consider the time problems of gathering genealogy information when scheduling presentations.

Oral History, Date Research, Genealogy

Handout 10

Directions: Choose one of the following:

I. Oral History. DUE: _____

Either alone or in pairs, you are to interview at least one person who remembers the decade. Using a tape recorder, you are to conduct an oral history interview of 15 minutes or more. You may ask any questions on any subject of the decade, although you may wish to concentrate on one subject or one idea such as from the ten history consensus statements.

When you are done with the interview, be ready to do the following:

1. Explain the backgrounds of a five-minute cutting from the interview and clarify what you learned. You may wish to use your paper.

2. Write a one- to three-page paper on your interview, especially on your choice of cutting. Be sure to include a response to a key question: "Does my interview confirm or deny what we have learned thus far about the decade?"

II. Date Research. DUE: _____

You are to find an issue of a magazine or newspaper of the decade. You may wish to focus on a day that interests you—a major event in the decade or in your life, for example, your birthday or an important family day such as a marriage. These artifacts (or microfilm copies) can be found in libraries, in the collections of your family and friends. Often you can make photocopies.

When you have examined the artifact, be ready to do the following:

1. Explain your choice—why you chose the artifact, its general nature, key stories and points that interested you, as well as the particular focus of your paper.

2. Write a one- to three-page paper on your research, not only on its general nature, but also on a question such as: "What does this artifact say in terms of what we have already learned about the decade?" You may want to use the history consensus statements.

III. Genealogy Research and Chart. DUE: _____

You are to trace your family on both maternal and paternal sides back to the beginning of the decade. For a satisfactory grade, you must include the direct line of your family with names, dates (birth and death) from you and your parents to those living when the decade began. For a higher grade, you must develop a family tree that includes some of the following: other relatives (aunts and uncles, cousins), occupations, geographical locations, cause of death: you may go back before the decade.

When you have completed your research, be ready to do the following:

1. Make a chart that clearly and visibly reveals your roots.

2. Be ready to discuss this chart and your research. Tell the class what you have learned about the decade and your family before and since the 1960s. Refer to such things as family size, names, occupations, mobility. Discuss family stories and individuals that reveal more than just statistics.

Suggestions: Oral history, family date research, and genealogy make excellent personal and family history. The charts, tapes, and your papers can be valuable to you and to your family. They are worth keeping and sharing. They may suggest ideas that you will pursue in your class project.

Student Writing Sample: Oral History

Interview with Debbie and Jim

The Sixties was a decade full of surprises. In our half hour interview with Debbie and Jim, we found interesting differences as well as similarities between the 1960s and today. Our five minute cut focused on four subjects that interested Mary and me: dating, dances, college education, and campus riots.

First of all, dating in the Sixties. In the films in class we learned that dating was important in the 1960s. In the interview we learned that it was improper for a girl to ask a boy out. Debbie and Jim stressed the fact that girls didn't ask boys out. Debbie mentioned that girls had to play a lot of "games" to get a certain boy to notice them. They both agreed that dating procedures are better now than then.

They also discussed the importance of going to dances. After the football games, the school held a dance and everybody went. There were many dances every school year. Not only were there dances at school, but there were other places in town with a live band every Friday night. So dances were popular social events in the Sixties. We had not noticed this in films or books in class. It was quite interesting to hear about this because it is different from today.

A college education was not pushed in the Sixties as much as we assumed it was. Only about fifty percent of Jim and Debbie's graduating class continued on to college. Many kids thought they could find a good job without college. Again, we had just assumed that attending college was stressed then as it is in today's society.

Finally, we heard about the anti-war rioting at the university campus. The students joined together as a mob and grew larger and larger and more and more out of control. The local police could no longer handle the situation as it progressed, so state troopers were called to the scene to keep control. From the class films and discussions, we had learned that rioting did occur, but it seemed more real and interesting to listen to someone talk about being in the middle of it.

We gained a lot of knowledge from our oral interview, and we feel good about this experience. We learned both new information and had a chance to review what we have learned, as well as to compare their lives with ours today.

Handout

Student Writing Sample: Date Research

Dateline: April 20, 1965

In the middle of the 1960s, one of the most turbulent decades this nation has ever experienced, many changes in the social, economic, and political structures took place. Many Americans look upon the year 1965 as the turning point, the year when crucial events affected the future of the United States.

One of these events changed my life, as I knew it. At 7:11 p.m., CST, a little girl was born in Iowa City, Iowa. She was named Leslie, and this auspicious occasion marked what I hope is the beginning of a great career.

Although this event did not take precedence over all other news items of the day, some "trivial" stories were printed. On that Tuesday, April 20, 1965, the University of Iowa's *Daily Iowan* ran a front page headline: "Reds Reject Unconditional Negotiations on Viet Nam." And in small print, I read, "Viet Cong Kills 9 More Americans." So 1965 was the year where the war in Viet Nam was escalated to the point where newspapers felt it deserved front-page treatment—instead of the usual obscure article here and there, next to "Dear Abby" or wedding announcements.

The use of "Reds" described the North Vietnamese government under Premier Pham Dong, and the repeated use of that phrase when referring to Viet Cong terrorists through the article reflects the lingering influence of the 1950s McCarthy Red Scare and the Cold War political philosophy.

Also on the front page, Rev. Martin Luther King, the great civil rights leader, got an injunction for a student march in Camden, Alabama, allowing him and other leaders to take students out of school for demonstrations.

The sports section was filled with upcoming events like the Iowa Hawkeye spring football drill the following week, as well as with local advertisements featuring Capezio leather shoes for $10 to $15 and a Stephen's Menswear suit for a mere $59.95. Those were the days . . .

The entertainment section featured Jack Lemmon in the comedy "How to Murder Your Wife," a fun-filled flick with Annette Funicello and Frankie Avalon frolicking in "Beach Blanket Bingo," and for you racy co-eds, "Diary of a Bachelor (Or How to Make It in the Business World)" was showing at the drive-in with a special double feature of "Under Age." Fun, fun.

The final page of the *Daily Iowan* is a full-page ad for a spring record sale with albums at $1.98. This sale featured such infamous albums as "Ambrosian Chants" and "The Red Army Ensemble." Obviously, these great deals wouldn't last long.

All in all, it wasn't a very exciting day for the rest of the world, but I'm sure the news of my birth livened up the paper. Oh well, what can one expect from a newspaper that only cost 10 cents? Not the *Washington Post* or the *New York Times*, I guess.

Lesson 22
History Options

Goal

This lesson will allow flexibility in the schedule. It may be used in a variety of ways.

Assignment

The first oral history playbacks will begin during Lesson 23—or later.

Procedure

1. This day may be spent completing the work of activity committees, such as making the handbook, presenting artifacts, completing the bulletin board, presenting the TV committee show.

2. The lesson could be spent with oral history interviews of local people about life in your community in the 1960s or about a special focus, such as the Vietnam Conflict. A volunteer student could conduct the interview as it was being taped.

3. The focus on artifacts can have a delightful twist if the instructor would make a series of photocopies of magazine advertisements from the 1960s—and other decades on the same subject, such as on automobiles. Bound decade magazines can be found in many local and university libraries for immediate photocopying. These photocopies can be used in a variety of challenging ways:

   a. Make overhead transparencies of these artifacts. Ask students to study each advertisement and then do a freewrite describing which artifacts are representative of the 1960s. Students share their freewrites; the instructor reveals the decade and comments as well.

   b. Use the same procedure as a warm-up with open class discussion on only two or three decade ads. Then divide the class into small groups, giving each group copies of the two or three ads that were discussed. First, the group members do a freewrite, then share their writing. The group selects a representative to share their writing with the class.

   c. Use the same procedure with open discussion. Divide the class into partners. Using only copies of four 1960s ads, distribute different ads to the partner groups, making sure that at least two groups have the same ad. Next, the partners discuss the ad and collaborate on a written artifact analysis. When they are finished, they should share their work with another partner group.

Additional Suggestion

The following sample artifact of high school rules and dress code makes a lively lesson in decade values, especially because students tend to stereotype the 1960s as a decade of rebellion. This artifact was included in the student handbook for 1967, the year of the hippie! It was approved by the student council, faculty, and school board in an Iowa community.

Handout

Sample Artifact

1967: Student Regulations: Boone High School Code of Conduct

1. All boys must wear belts in their proper place; that is, at the waistline.
2. T-shirts are not to be worn without a top shirt.
3. Shirts must be worn buttoned with the exception of the top button.
4. No levis will be permitted at school dances or school parties.
5. During regular school hours and summer school, boys and girls will not be permitted to wear Bermuda shorts or clothes of a similar type.
6. Shirttails are to be worn inside the trousers unless tailored to be worn at the belt line.
7. Heel clips will not be allowed on boys' shoes.
8. Girls are expected to keep their skirts the length of the current styles. At the present time, we are informed that the skirt must not be shorter than the top of the kneecap.
9. During the regular school hours boys are not to wear a sweat shirt without a dress type shirt. Girls are not to wear sweat shirts.
10. Girls are not to come to school with their hair in pins or curlers.
11. According to the By-laws of the Boys' High School Athletic Association, any student whose habits and/or conduct during the school year or during the summer months are such as to make him unworthy to represent the ideals, principles and standards of his school and the athletic association shall be ineligible to participate in organized athletics. In Boone Junior-Senior High School the purpose and intent of the above policy will be observed at all extra-curricular activities.
12. CIGARETTES ARE NOT TO BE CARRIED IN SCHOOL BY ANY STUDENT.
13. All boys are to wear their shirt collars down.
14. Students who are smoking or those who are under the influence of alcoholic beverages not acceptable for use by minors while under the jurisdiction of the school will be subject to disciplinary action. Students are considered being under school supervision during regular school hours or participating in school activities in Boone or other towns and when using school-sponsored transportation.
15. All rules concerning drinking and smoking apply to students at Goeppinger Field and school parking lot as well as all other school property.

16. Any student whose personal appearance is such that it creates a condition in our school that is a detraction to our student body, and a distracting factor, will be required to appear before the Student Citizenship Committee.

17. A student citizens' group appointed by the Student Council and Student Congress will relay students' reactions to the administration in reference to usual procedure in dress, personal grooming, etc. The purpose of these groups is to help keep the standards of the student body in step with current trends and yet keep Boone Junior-Senior High School a school that students, faculty, and community can be proud to represent. Any new fads will be brought to the attention of the group to determine whether students and faculty members are to accept the fad in the school.

18. All faculty members are expected to assist in the enforcement of any of the above regulations in which an infraction occurs. If any student fails to observe the above regulations, he may be dropped from school in three days and if the situation isn't settled during the period of suspension, it will be necessary for the student to appear before the Board of Education for readmittance.

19. The above regulations drawn up by the Administration, Student Council, and Student Congress were approved by the Board of Education and became effective April 16, 1962.

> Student Congress
> Student Council
> Faculty of Junior-Senior High
> Board of Education

Lessons 23–24
Oral History and
Date Research

Goal

Understanding oral history and date research as methods of evaluating a culture and testing assumptions that come from reading or small-group discussions.

Materials

1. Audiotape or videotape recorder-player.

2. Copies of the composite statement "Class Consensus on History Small Groups." See Lesson 21.

Procedure

1. Review the concept of oral history as a tool for understanding a period and getting to meet primary sources—real people who lived in the period and remember what it meant to them.

2. Ask the students to refer to the class consensus statement as they listen to the playback.

3. Each student (or the partners) should describe the interview, play back about five minutes, and tell what they learned, using their papers if they wish. Invite class comments and questions. If the tape is especially good, the students should be encouraged to play more.

4. When the oral history students are finished, move on to the date researchers. Ask them to write their dates on the board and then describe their experience. Encourage them to refer to their papers and to show the artifacts or photocopies.

5. Be sure to collect papers *after* each presentation of oral history or date research.

6. Lessons 23–24 could be varied with suggestions from Lesson 21.

7. Remind genealogy students to bring charts on day 25. Encourage them to bring family artifacts: birth certificates, baby books, photographs.

Lesson 25
Genealogy

Goal

Completion of oral history, date research, genealogy.

Materials

Audiotape or videotape player or both.

Procedure

1. Complete any remaining oral history or date research presentations.

2. Begin genealogy presentations. Remind the students to discuss their research and what they learned about their families—the information that's on their family trees and also how they found or did not find the information. What does their family tree say about their family and the 1960s, about today, and about the time before the 1960s—everything from names and family size to occupations and mobility? The 1960s began a dramatic change in the nuclear family—divorce. Is this revealed in the charts? Ask students to refer to family stories and artifacts.

Later, a bulletin board display of these family trees is effective reinforcement, as well as recognition of superior efforts.

Additional and Alternative Suggestions

1. A final discussion or freewrite on oral history, date research, and family trees would help the students arrive at a larger understanding: What did you learn about America and the 1960s from your efforts and the class efforts on oral history, date research, and genealogy?

2. Tombstone research. Students might select decade tombstones in the local cemetery for theoretical analysis and do obituary research, using the newspapers and microfilms in the local library. Tombstone research should be suggested as a possible term project, for example, on the value difference between 1960s tombstones and tombstones of another decade or century. This research would involve close study of epitaphs and art work, sizes and shapes, theories about the living who made the tombstones, and their attitudes about life and death. Encourage partner projects that include videotaping.

Lesson 26
The Term Project

Goal

Orientation to the term project.

Materials

1. Handout 11: "Suggestions for Term Projects."

2. Handout 12: "Term Project Proposal."

3. A class library of term paper handbooks and stylebooks, either locally prepared or commercial.

Assignment

The due date for the term project proposal should be assigned. It is suggested that the date come before Lesson 40 as part of the first evaluation period.

Procedure

1. Review the purpose of the term project proposal and note that it is an important part of the course for student development, individualization, and evaluation. Students can work alone or with partners on this in-depth study that will reveal their understanding of American Humanities.

2. Give each student copies of Handouts 11 and 12.

3. Explain that the project will be handled step by step with ample planning time so that the students can produce a project they will be proud of.

4. Refer to the Ten Steps to a Successful Project, written on the board:

    1. Orientation

    2. Research, choosing and limiting a topic

    3. Submitting the proposal

    4. First conference

    5. Taking notes, being organized, building a focus

    6. Submitting a progress report: narrowed topic

    7. Second conference

8. **Assembling notes and materials**
9. **Writing rough and final drafts, making the final outline**
10. **Submitting the project**

5. Review the various suggestions on Handout 11. Be sure to stress that the students should remember that the project is not in art or literature or history, but in American Humanities. Stress that they must review their interests and strengths (although they may wish to pursue something that could become a strength) and that they should decide what type of project would be best for them.

6. Review the handout on "Term Project Proposals" (Handout 12). Note the due date: _____ . Stress that to do a project one must have a research plan, materials, people to work with no matter how interesting the subject, and evidence of a plan so that step 4, the first conference, can be useful. Evaluation for the first period of the course will include the success of this proposal.

7. Orientation is over. Now the students should prepare for steps 2, 3, and 4.

The next lessons will involve very little homework so that students can work on the proposal.

Additional Suggestions

1. Encourage preconference meetings. Help the students brainstorm. Encourage partner projects, with the reservation that the students make clear their individual and group responsibilities.

2. Encourage collaborative projects where two to five students develop a presentation or performance, a product such as a video-play or documentary or a model such as an architectural display.

3. Before and during the periods of the first conference, some students will ask to change their projects. This is an important time for them, so let them get hold of what they really want to do. But insist on their making a new proposal so that everyone is clear about the new topic.

4. Establish a recognition system. Display projects in the school library. Have a traveling "Oscar" for the best project of the year. This "Oscar" can be made by a student or an art class, or it can be purchased from a local business that makes trophies. Place it in the school trophy case! Be ready to announce the award to the school and community news-papers. Offer outstanding research projects to local public and historical libraries.

5. After the first year, refer to previous projects and interdisciplinary ideas.

6. For additional ideas about the teacher's role as an integral part of the humanities project, see the article that follows: "The Natural: The English Teacher as Humanities Teacher." You might consider sharing this essay with the students.

The Natural: The English Teacher as Humanities Teacher

Brooke Workman

Last summer I visited with my brother-in-law who is in charge of the East Coast division of a large computer corporation. I asked my favorite question for business leaders, "What are you looking for in your hiring of young people?" His answer was immediate, "We want somebody who can communicate, somebody who can think creatively."

"Now wait a minute," I said. "I thought you guys were looking for the computer hackers, the specialists." He shook his head. "No, we train them for our special needs. But the world is changing fast—and we need people who can change with it." Then I did a quick flashback to a *Newsweek* article that quoted a robotics expert who said that one-third of all jobs today will be replaced by robots in 1993.

Ernest Boyer recently warned educators that beefing up traditional courses is not enough to relate students to the larger world. Instead, he called for "a new interdisciplinary vision" to connect the disciplines. And he stressed that students must make those connections themselves. His specific recommendations is a "Senior Independent Project" that draws upon various disciplines.

At first, recommendations seem to clash with realities. In the last ten years, the high school curriculum has responded to tight budgets, declining enrollment, and the cry of "Back to Basics"—as well as a recent appeal for increased high order thinking skills. Realities have led to larger classes, more textbooks, and fewer electives. And the senior term paper (or term paper somewhere, for God's sake) has reared its familiar head.

Frankenstein assemblage of secondary sources, whether it be initiated in a social studies or English classroom. A footnote here, a bibliography there. A unit perhaps, but not integrated into a total program. College preparation perhaps, but seldom for the larger world of creative thought, for vision.

Ernest Boyer is really talking about us—English teachers. We certainly meet all the qualifications of a visionary. What other teachers accept the responsibility of reading and writing—the basis of all learning—let alone speaking, listening, and high order thinking skills? And from a realistic standpoint, he must mean us because school boards and administrators see us as naturals for senior projects, term papers, or whatever you call them. We reach all the students, usually every year.

In many ways English teachers are naturals for initiating experiments in interdisciplinary learning, whether we work alone or with teams from inside or outside the department, using the talents of the students and the resources of the community. And certainly we are interdisciplinary teachers. What American literature teacher, for example, does not discuss history or does not relate the difference between the film version of a short story and the literary text? Which of us has not enriched classes with music or art or photography? We understand that the world is not departmentalized.

But again, how can we avoid thirty students rushing off in thirty directions? In 1968, our English Department at West High School decided to experiment with American humanities. We began with a study of a decade that would relate students to parents, to the community, to American culture. This elective ran in one direction, but its parts were always related to the whole. For

example, we began with dominant values of American culture. Then we moved to history, social history, oral history, family history; next to literature, film, radio; finally art, architecture, dance, music. By 1985, we had given our students a choice of 1920s, 1930s, 1945–60, or 1960s for twenty-four weeks of study.

The methods for discovering the whole through analysis of the artifacts or the parts included speeches on values in contemporary artifacts, position papers on decade artifacts, such as best sellers, small group consensus discussions on historical theories, teaching a painting, written comparisons of modern and decade houses, and performances and analysis of period plays. But, according to student evaluations, the best part of the course was *the project.*

Here we discovered what Boyer meant by "a new interdisciplinary vision." Through a ten-step procedure, from project proposal through two individual conferences to final presentation/product, we discovered why this kind of project was more successful than the old term paper. We saw how a total course reinforced the individual's search for connections. And we saw extraordinary products, creative extensions of student talents, ones which would have been difficult to achieve in other settings.

Let's examine four American Humanities projects.

Dennis was a talented musician, a member of a 1930s section. He played in the school jazz band, the orchestra, the pep band. His world was tied to performance, though he had begun to study music theory. His project proposal was as expected: he wanted to do something with 1930s

music, maybe jazz, maybe a term paper on a composer. Though I have no formal training in music, I told Dennis how much I liked Aaron Copland's work. We discussed what we had learned about the Depression and Regionalism in literature and art and music.

By the second conference, Dennis announced that he had decided to concentrate on Copland. "Why write a term paper?" I asked. "Music is music. Why not write a piece in the style of Copland?" Dennis smiled. "I talked with Mr. DeSalme about that," he said. Mr. DeSalme was his music theory teacher. So Dennis wrote "Springtime in Iowa in the 1930s"—and he directed the school orchestra's performance, after an introductory discussion of his project. Today Dennis holds a doctorate in music. Recently he has been doing arrangements for the U.S. Army Herald Trumpets which perform at the White House.

Susan enjoyed art, though her college prep schedule allowed little room for such luxuries. Her class on the 1945–60 period soon discovered that not everything was like "Happy Days"; she was intrigued with both the Beat poets and the Abstract Expressionist painters. Her proposal was ambitious—she was going to paint five paintings in the style of such artists as Robert Motherwell, Mark Rothko, Josef Albers, Willem de Kooning, and Jackson Pollock. She was going to lecture to the class on each and on Abstact Expressionism.

Having had but one Exploring Art course as an undergraduate but from then on a passion for art museums, I encouraged her ambition. I suggested that she consult with our art teacher. And we talked about why an Eisenhower era should breed Kerouacs and de Koonings, Arthur Millers, and

Motherwells. Finally, presentation day arrived. The room was filled with huge Jack-the-Dripper canvases. And Susan launched forth with her lecture. Today, Susan is an artist in California.

Then came Jim, a junior deeply puzzled about Iowa farmers in the 1930s. For Jim, Iowa farmers were quiet folk, not rebels, certainly not radicals, but as he read his history, his Steinbeck, his Sandburg, he began to understand that the Depression was an extraordinary period. And so was Milo Reno, leader of the radical farmers of Iowa that nearly lynched judges in bankruptcy court. But Jim was not satisfied with the textbook snippets.

Jim's proposal was a classic. He would read 1930s newspapers, he would read the Reno Papers at the University of Iowa Library, and he would go around the state and interview people that knew Milo Reno. (Jim had been inspired by our oral history section.) And he did—all those things, producing a first-rate primary source term paper which reminded me of my master's thesis. Jim went on to Harvard, ran for Congress, and wrote a published history of the Iowa Democratic Party.

Finally, there is Aaron, a recent graduate of a 1960s class. Aaron starred in all the school plays. At first, I thought he might follow the path of previous school thespians who had written term papers on dramatists or performed and then analyzed cuttings from decade plays. When I read his artifact film analysis of *Georgy Girl*, I could see great comic talent. I could also see that he was intrigued with the special craziness of the 1960s, a time of revolution in the arts. In the first conference, we reviewed his proposal to study the Absurd Theatre. "Why not reveal the 1960s in your own Absurd play, maybe something like Edward Albee's plays?" I suggested. Aaron took the bait, first reading about the Absurd Theatre, then plays by Albee, Heller, Kopit, and French writers.

Aaron's one act, "The Artist's Conception," led to NCTE recognition and to eventual publication, thanks to our language arts coordinator. Two years later, our American Humanities Seminar performed his absurd play for local cable television—and Aaron came home on vacation from the University of Pennsylvania to instruct and inspire the class.

Dennis, Susan, Jim, Aaron. They and all the others—from Albert performing his Gershwin preludes to Debbie's study of 1920s cigarette ads for women, from Linda's original research on the controversy over building Iowa City's 1939 high school to Stephen's ten projector/computer driven slide show on Elvis Presley—were just waiting for the humanities. They found the natural environment for their talents: the English classroom.

Brooke Workman teaches at West High School, Iowa City, Iowa.

"The Natural: The English Teacher as Humanities Teacher" by Brooke Workman first appeared in *English Journal*, (74) 7. © 1985 NCTE. Used by permission.

Suggestions for Term Projects

Nature of the Project

Your research project, whether it be a term paper or a class presentation, should pursue some basic American Humanities questions:

1. What does your project say about the values of Americans in that decade? Also: What does it say in relation to our society today?

2. Does the topic represent a major or minor current of the decade?

3. Does your topic relate to what is being studied in class? Or does it explore new territory, an area that is special to you and would help the class understand this facet of our culture?

4. How does your particular subject relate to the total culture at the time? For example, if your project is interdisciplinary, a project largely in art or music should also relate to history or even literature.

General Interests

What are your general interests: music, art, literature, sports, film, dancing, history, politics, architecture, sculpture, radio, television, fashions, education, business, advertising, science, crime, inventions, religion, photography, popular culture (for example, comics, toys, games, fads)?

Type of Project

A. You may do a term paper: seven to ten pages. In high school classes, this project is especially valuable for college-bound students. You will learn to research various libraries, examine varied materials, develop techniques for narrowing your topic, develop an outline and note cards and a bibliography, organize, synthesize. Copies of term papers will be on file, and a class library of handbooks and stylebooks will be available, although you will be encouraged to buy one of these at a local bookstore.

Take chances. Steer away from Frankenstein term papers—piecing together dead parts of secondary sources such as encyclopedias. Look for topics that relate to primary sources, people and decade artifacts, about your school and community.

B. You may do a creative project that also may involve a presentation. You may want a partner for such ambitious projects. Possibilities:

    1. A video or film based on a narrowed topic

    2. A slide show on a theme—such as local architecture or history

3. A series of drawings for discussion or instruction on such things as fashion or dancing or architecture

4. A photographic display based on a photographer or a central theme

5. A study of genealogy or local cemeteries, using slides, video, oral history, or charts and scrapbooks

6. A play or novel or series of stories in the style of a decade writer

7. A journal by a contemporary such as a teenager or a soldier

8. A musical composition and performance based on the study of individual artists or groups

9. A display of student-made art work such as paintings or sculpture in the style of a decade artist

10. A synchronization study: art slides or video with music and literature; for example, student poetry that defines the mind and work of a decade artist

11. An architecture tour of the community, based on theme or theory, such as decade dream houses

12. An oral history study: tapes, transcriptions pursuing a theme

13. A construction to reveal the decade: interior decorating, a dream house, a famous decade building

14. Writing a children's book based on the study of a decade writer or writers, with art work

15. A 1960s style show in the school theater

Additional Suggestions for American Humanities Projects

1. Compare one week of your teenage world with that of a relative who lived during the decade.

2. Take one or more bestsellers, Pulitzer Prize winners, or controversial books and examine them as artifacts.

3. Compare a decade high school yearbook with the same school's most recent production.

4. Study children's books of the decade with a particular focus— racism, sexism, definition of the family.

5. Decide what you think makes a person an American hero or heroine. Then analyze one from the decade. Compare one with a hero or heroine of today, such as two film stars, two professional sports figures.

6. Do a comparative or evolutionary study of one product, such as automobiles or cigarettes, in magazine advertising—then and now. Make photocopies for analysis.

7. Analyze a series of "Dear Abby" columns. What troubled 1960s America?

8. Study a decade comic strip for a month in terms of decade artifact analysis.

9. Focus on an event: 1968 Olympics, Bay of Pigs, Woodstock.

10. What makes a book controversial, for example, Ralph Nader's *Unsafe at Any Speed* or Kurt Vonnegut's *Slaughterhouse-Five?*

11. What was all the controversy about Cassius Clay/Muhammad Ali, Malcolm X, Timothy Leary?

12. What really was a hippie? Use oral history, books, magazines.

13. Find lyrics of popular songs that revolve around one theme such as love, war, happiness, or teenagers.

14. What does Bryan's *Friendly Fire*, Power's *Diana: The Making of a Terrorist*, or Lederer's *A Nation of Sheep* say about America in the 1960s?

15. Study a sensational crime, for example, the Charles Manson story or Truman Capote's account of murder in Kansas in his *In Cold Blood.*

16. Analyze an election. Why did Kennedy beat Nixon?

17. Analyze dreams and utopias. Study decade science fiction and predictions of the future.

18. Focus on film or television. Do an in-depth study of a program or film that was a Nielsen favorite or a box office sensation.

19. Analyze the influence of the Beatles—a British group.

20. What is a radical? What values did SDS, the Weathermen, the Black Panthers challenge?

21. Study 1960s fashions—the rise of blue jeans, men's and women's clothing, the bathing suit, shoes, hair styles.

22. Study humor, jokes, humorists (such as Lenny Bruce or Mort Sahl). What was funny in the 1960s?

23. Study one author (Edward Albee or Norman Mailer), one painter (Andy Warhol or Andrew Wyeth), one architect (Eero Saarinen or Buckminster Fuller), one musician (Bob Dylan or Barbra Streisand), or one musical (*Camelot* or *Hair*).

24. Compare a politician, then and now.

25. What was happening in your community or state that reveals the 1960s?

Term Project Proposal

DUE: _____

Name, Period _____

I. Subject or Title:

II. Research Plan: What are the first things you plan to do? Where are the materials you plan to study? What aspect of the general subject do you plan to study? Will there be sufficient materials? (Use the space below or a separate sheet.)

III. Tentative Outline: On a separate sheet, outline the features of your subject that you expect to cover. If you feel you cannot now plan a rough outline, be ready to discuss project organization at the first conference. A working outline will be due at the second conference.

IV. Bibliography: On a separate sheet or on the back of this sheet, list materials that you plan to investigate and use (for example, titles of books, magazines, audiovisual materials, plus names and qualifications of resource persons).

V. Conferences: First _____   Second _____

Lessons 27–40
Popular Culture

Students need to know a wide range of strategies for approaching symbol systems and to learn methods of analyzing the logic and argument of these systems. Electronic technologies supplement and alter literacy as it has been traditionally defined.

The English Coalition: Democracy through Language (37)

Lessons 27–28
Television

Goal

Understanding how values are transmitted through the popular culture of television.

Materials

1. A VCR and a videotape of a 1960s program. Decade television programs are readily available in video stores and bookstores, as well as on TV reruns. Also check video rental businesses and local library collections.

2. Handout 4: "Dominant American Values."

3. History consensus statements.

4. See "Teacher Notes: One Approach to Studying Television" at the end of this lesson.

Procedure

1. Remind the students that the next lessons will require almost no homework so that they can work on term project proposals.

2. Ask the students to take out their dominant values handout, as well as their more recent history consensus statements.

3. Write the following basic historical statistics on the board—or make a copy for each student.

Year	TV Households, %	Multiple Sets, %	Color Sets, %
1950	9.0	1.0	0
1955	64.5	2.9	0
1959	85.9	9.6	0.06
1960	87.1	12.0	0.7
1965	92.6	19.4	4.9
1969	95.0	30.9	32.0

Source: *Trends in Television* (New York: Television Bureau of Advertising, October 1989), 3–4.

4. Ask the students to do a freewrite interpreting the data. Then ask the students to share their responses. Ask them to reflect on the major

media before 1946—radio and films, as well as print. Ask them to interpret not only the rise of TV (especially color), but also how TV differs from radio.

5. Remind the students of their previous paper on TV values. Now we are going to focus on 1960s TV and values. Does 1960s TV reveal both the dominant values and specific decade concerns?

6. Ask the students to name some 1960s TV programs. Remind them that the Top Ten TV shows are especially successful in molding Americans. Put on the board some of the following top-rated shows, according to the Nielsen polls: "Ed Sullivan," "Beverly Hillbillies," "Bonanza," "Gunsmoke," "My Three Sons," "Andy Griffith Show," "Flintstones," "Star Trek," "The Lucy Show," "Gilligan's Island," "Flipper," "What's My Line?," "Dick Van Dyke Show," "Mission Impossible," "Rowan and Martin's Laugh-In," "Hawaii Five-0," "Mod Squad," "Bill Cosby Show," "Brady Bunch," "Sesame Street."

7. Remind the students of the fishbowling poll, 1960 versus 1980, and how TV became a major influence in teenagers' lives. Why?

8. Use the stop-start, freewrite procedure with the 1960s video artifact. Ask key questions: What dominant American values are emerging? What attitudes are revealed about success, freedom, patriotism, moral orientation, sex roles, concern for conformity to law, the family? Ask the students to look closely at the sets and the clothing? Does anything seem particular to the 1960s? Check the history consensus statements. What about the music track, laugh machines, camera techniques, the number of seconds on one focus? What is the final meaning of the episode?

Additional Suggestions

1. Invite resource people who lived in the 1960s to share their expertise, to watch the video with the class and respond to it from their background. Note: You may want to videotape this interview. Possible questions:

    a. Do you remember your first TV set, the shift from a black and white set to color?

    b. What did it look like? How large was the screen?

    c. Where was it located in your home? Why?

    d. Did you have a favorite program at different points in the decade?

    e. Do you remember a specific program and overall concerns: the Kennedy assassination and funeral, the Beatles on TV, space exploration, civil rights marches, student protests, the impact of Vietnam news?

2. You may wish to extend the television section with a film on the impact of the media and a follow-up discussion. Suggestions: (a) the late 1960s films on Marshall McLuhan and the medium as the message, for example, *Communication Revolution*. (b) Bill Moyers's *The Public Mind: Images and Reality in America: Consuming Images* on the power of media manipulation. (See text that follows this lesson: "Teacher Notes: One Approach to Studying Television.")

3. Television can be an excellent term project, for example, on the role of the family, of women, of minorities. Partners can develop a video project based on a decade program or a concept.

Teacher Notes: One Approach to Studying Television

Background

The impact of television became obvious by the 1960s. It invaded our homes, our schools, our lives. In the 1960s Marshall McLuhan suggested how this medium would become the cultural message, how the electronic world differed from the world of print—books, newspapers, magazines. In the late 1970s, Neil Postman theorized about the impact on the first generation of TV children in *Teaching as a Conserving Activity* (1979).

According to recent statistics, thirteen years of school take 2,340 days and 11,500 hours. Thirteen years of TV watching for the average student take 15,000 hours (plus another 15,000 hours with radio, records or tapes, and movies). Professor Postman, a student of American culture and television, says that TV became the "1st Curriculum" and school became the "2nd Curriculum."

1. TV is image-centered; words are secondary; abstractions and ideas are not essential. School requires reflection, not just engaged emotion.

2. TV is not hierarchical. It is for everyone with no prerequisites. School builds on previous learning. It has a sense of history, of continuity.

3. TV does not require memory or lead to future satisfaction; attendance is its own reward. TV does not ask questions; it is experienced at home, allows continuous freedom of choice. School requires group norms, expects responses, leads to future gratification.

4. TV immediacy is short—modules broken up by ads every eight to ten minutes, 1,000 ads a week, which break concentration, with unrelated parables of modern life (beer for peer

group acceptance, mouthwash for social acceptance). School requires extended discussion of complex human problems.

The 1960s produced a generation more present-centered, more interested in passive gratification, in feeling more than reason, a "do your own thing" individualism, yet caught up in simplistic messages, with attention-span problems, with organizing, writing, and oral skills.

An Approach

To understand the impact of TV on 1960s children, as well as those of today, the instructor might use Bill Moyers's *Images and Reality in America: Consuming Images,* and then ask the students to freewrite and discuss their responses to the following questions:

1. Imagine there is no television and no radio. What would the world be like? What would school be like? How would people learn about the world? (Note: America from 1607 to 1920!)

2. Then imagine radio is invented. What would the world be like now?

3. Next imagine that television is invented. What would the world be like now? How does television differ from oral traditions, print (books and magazines), radio, and films at a movie theater?

4. In the 1960s, Marshall McLuhan wrote, "When man lives in an electric environment, his nature is transformed." How might TV change a student?

5. How is TV different from school?

6. Suggest a theory about the molding of the 1960s children by TV.

Lessons 29–31
Movies

Goal

Understanding how values are transmitted through the popular culture medium of film, Hollywood films.

Materials

1. One feature-length film of the decade. Videotapes of decade films are easily obtained from city libraries and rental businesses, as well as from universities and educational agencies. Suggestions:

    a. *To Kill a Mockingbird* (1962)

    b. *Dr. Strangelove* (1964)

    c. *In the Heat of the Night* (1967)

    d. *The Odd Couple* (1968)

    e. *Easy Rider* (1969)

    f. *Butch Cassidy and the Sundance Kid* (1969)

2. Handout 13: "Film as Artifact Analysis."

Assignment

The students should be asked to take notes, refer to the dominant values sheet (Handout 4) and the class consensus sheet, and write a one- to three-page analysis of the film as decade artifact.

Procedure

1. Review the idea that television and now films are means of transmitting values.

2. Discuss the assignment and use of the dominant values and class consensus handouts. Distribute Handout 13, "Film as Artifact Analysis." Tell the students the due date: _____ .

3. Remind the students that these films may suggest term projects and that this three-day study also allows them time to work on the term project proposal.

4. Suggest projects: a study of an actor, director, a famous film, why Americans liked big musicals (*The Sound of Music*) or nostalgia (such as

Bogart or Chaplin films)—all topics that could be developed into term papers of media projects such as a James Bond-type film.

Additional Suggestions

If time and budget permit, you may wish to use more than three days for films. Film study should work for variety as well as for entertainment: documentary (*Woodstock*), cool hero dramas (*Goldfinger*), science fiction (*2001—A Space Odyssey*), strictly teenage (*Beach Party*), humorous-controversial (*Guess Who's Coming to Dinner?*). A valuable introductory film to the 1960s: *Hollywood, the Dream Factory.*

Film as Artifact Analysis

DUE: _____

Sample of Student Paper

Easy Rider: A Sixties Artifact

Easy Rider, released in 1969, is remembered as a youth classic of the Sixties counterculture. The clothes, speech, and mannerisms of the main characters are obviously those of rebellious young people. But more than these superficial aspects reveal that the film suggests major value changes that were occurring at this time.

First, the treatment of the subject of this film is different from the youth-oriented films prior to the decade. Previously, the youth acted as young adults who were developing the values and mores that their parents already possessed. But in *Easy Rider* the youth were searching for their own attitudes, not those imposed on them. Hollywood was recognizing the inherent differences between the generations. Previous attempts, such as *Rebel Without a Cause*, did not show radically shocking or different behavior, just what was considered the naivete or frivolity of youth. Instead of siding with the rebellious, as *Easy Rider* does, previous films showed, in the end, that the adults and their conservative ways were ultimately right.

The heroes in *Easy Rider* were unlike those of the past. The image that comes to mind when a character is described as a social drop-out, a drug user, and a drifter is not a positive one. Yet *Easy Rider* takes these "unworthy" characters and shows to the public that they are not evil. The traditional hero, although sometimes a womanizer or heavy drinker, was at least fairly mainstream. The heroes of *Easy Rider*, Wyatt and Billy, were not mainstream America. They break from traditional hero definition—a break which was finally made more possible by the more relaxed atmosphere of the 1960s.

Finally, the movie is innovative by its ending. The heroes lose. They admit that they "blew it," and they are blown away. It has happened before, but usually the movie would end with a sort of optimism. *Easy Rider* ends with anger. On the other hand, something which makes this movie distinctive is the ambiguity of the "heroes." Most movies have cops and robbers, and the audience definitely knows which side should win. But because of radically different national opinions in the Sixties, the red-necks of the South and the conservatives seem to win. Or do they? The way that this movie acknowledges that not everyone can be on the same side is a distinctive quality new in the decade.

Easy Rider, like many movies since, shows the difference in attitudes which is inevitable between generations. The movie was a significant change from the traditional Hollywood stereotypes and plots, and, therefore, it is an important artifact of the sixties, a decade of change.

Lesson 32
Literature: Bestsellers and Position Papers

Goal

Understanding how values are transmitted and reinforced through the popular culture medium of the bestseller.

Materials

1. Class copies of bestsellers.

2. Handout 14: "1960s Bestsellers."

3. Handout 15: "Position Paper and Defense Day."

4. Handout 17: "A Collaborative Student Position Paper: Bestsellers as Artifacts."

Assignment

1. Television, films, popular books—all are artifacts and reinforce values.

2. Ask the students to describe recent bestsellers and to theorize why they are so popular, though often not taught in schools. Suggestion: Find a list of top bestsellers in a Sunday edition of a major newspaper such as *The New York Times*. Read one of these books before this lesson, and theorize why this might have broad national appeal.

3. Distribute Handout 14 on 1960s bestsellers. Ask the students if any titles sound familiar. Many of these books became movies. You may wish to list student responses on the board.

4. Give each student the handouts on the position paper and defense day (Handout 15) and the student writing sample (Handout 17). The position paper will be two to four typed pages.

5. Review the handouts and writing sample. Then describe the bestsellers available. You may wish to have all the students write on the same book—or on more than one book—for one or more defense days. Consider the length and difficulty as well. Suggestions:

Black Like Me (1960), by John Howard Griffin

To Kill a Mockingbird (1960), by Harper Lee

Nigger: An Autobiography (1964), by Dick Gregory

The Chosen (1967), by Chaim Potok

Slaughterhouse-Five (1969), by Kurt Vonnegut, Jr.

I Know Why the Caged Bird Sings (1969), by Maya Angelou

Love Story (1970), by Erich Segal

Note: You may wish to use a 1950s book such as J. D. Salinger's *The Catcher in the Rye* (1951), which was very popular with young people in the 1960s.

Alternate and Additional Suggestions

1. Try the collaborative approach: two students work together, write the paper together, defend it together. This is an exciting approach—and it cuts down on the paper load!

2. Alternate Handout 14, "1960s Novels and Nonfiction as Artifacts," offers additional choices of popular and critically acclaimed novels.

3. Again this is a likely project topic, such as a comparison with decade and modern bestsellers, or a major work on minorities, for example, *Autobiography of Malcolm X* (1965). A study of decade Pulitzer Prize winners can be valuable as well. Finally, a focus on a popular book for both children and adults can open up a valuable cultural subject. Example: The revival of J. R. R. Tolkien's 1938 novel, *The Hobbit*.

4. Continue the small-group discussion approach with four small groups—chairs, secretaries-recorders, observers—much like the history consensus group. This alternate could involve from two to four days, on two to four different books. Set three goals that require individual and group notes to be given to the instructor:

   a. Describe the plot in at least eight sentences.

   b. Make a list of eight examples from the book that mark it as an artifact of the time in which it was written (for example, names of characters, slang, references to events and activities of the decade, period values).

   c. The group should arrive at one consensus statement about what this artifact says about the period. The chair and the secretary-recorder should work with the group in making and recording the group's consensus on each of the three points or goals.

1960s Bestsellers

Handout
14

Note: An excellent source on bestsellers is *80 Years of Best Sellers, 1895–1975*, by Alice Payne Hackett (1977), from which the information below is taken. The following selection is from the top ten of each year.

Year	Fiction	Nonfiction
1960	*Hawaii*, James Michener	*May This House Be Safe from Tigers*, Alexander King
1961	*To Kill a Mockingbird*, Harper Lee	*A Nation of Sheep*, William J. Lederer
1962	*Ship of Fools*, Katherine Anne Porter	*Travels with Charley*, John Steinbeck
1963	*The Group*, Mary McCarthy	*Profiles in Courage*, John F. Kennedy
1964	*The Spy Who Came in from the Cold*, John Le Carré	*In His Own Write*, John Lennon
1965	*Up the Down Staircase*, Bel Kaufman	*A Gift of Prophecy: The Phenomenal Jean Dixon*, Ruth Montgomery
1966	*Valley of the Dolls*, Jacqueline Susann	*In Cold Blood*, Truman Capote
1967	*The Chosen*, Chaim Potok	*Death of a President*, William Manchester
1968	*Airport*, Arthur Hailey	*Listen to the Warm*, Rod McKuen
1969	*The Godfather*, Mario Puzo	*The Peter Principle*, Laurence J. Peter and Raymond Hull
1970	*Love Story*, Erich Segal	*Everything You Always Wanted to Know about Sex but Were Afraid to Ask*, David Reuben

1960s Novels and Nonfiction as Artifacts

1960   *Advise and Consent,* Allen Drury
       The Waste Makers, Vance Packard
       Rabbit, Run, John Updike

1961   *Stranger in a Strange Land,* Robert Heinlein
       Franny and Zooey, J. D. Salinger
       The Winter of Our Discontent, John Steinbeck

1962   *Another Country,* James Baldwin
       The Reivers, William Faulkner
       One Flew Over the Cuckoo's Nest, Ken Kesey
       Silent Spring, Rachel Carson

1963   *The Learning Tree,* Gordon Parks
       Cat's Cradle, Kurt Vonnegut, Jr.

1964   *The Rector of Justin,* Louis Auchincloss
       I Never Promised You a Rose Garden, Hannah Green
       The Keepers of the House, Shirley Ann Grau

1965   *Hotel,* Arthur Hailey
       Manchild in the Promised Land, Claude Brown

1966   *The Fixer,* Bernard Malamud

1967   *The Outsiders,* S. E. Hinton
       Rosemary's Baby, Ira Levin

1968   *House Made of Dawn,* N. Scott Momaday

1969   *The Andromeda Strain,* Michael Crichton
       Lisa, Bright and Dark, John Neufeld

Position Paper and Defense Day

DUE: _____

The Position Paper

1. The position paper is just that: you develop a single position about what you have read, a narrowed focus that is developed with concrete examples. The position is *your* position. Note: You may collaborate with a partner. On defense day, the entire small group will study your paper and try to find your position.

2. The paper must be two to four typed pages. It must be typed so that it may be photocopied for all the students in your group if your paper is chosen for defense day. Every student will receive a copy of the paper the day before defense day.

3. The possibilities for positions are nearly unlimited, though you will need to remember that you are examining the book as a decade artifact. What does it say about America in your decade? What values are revealed? Does your paper reflect a dominant value or a consensus statement of the history small group? You may want to compare the book with today.

4. Whether you are chosen or not for defense day, all papers will focus on at least three criteria: (a) clarity of position, (b) organization and concrete support of your position, (c) sound mechanics of writing. Don't let errors in proofreading, spelling, punctuation, capitalization, run-on sentences, and fragments distract readers from your ideas.

5. Don't be afraid to take chances in a strong position, a strong style, and original approach. But also work on concrete support—lines and examples that prove your point.

6. Don't use the title of the book for your paper. Let the title suggest or reflect your position.

7. Remember that your readers are your classmates. They read the book, too. They are your friends.

Defense Day

1. Two papers will be chosen for defense day; the rest will be evaluated by the instructor. Everyone will receive a copy of the defense day papers.

2. You will read the two papers overnight and write on them what you like about them, what questions you have, what might be improved.

3. Be prepared for defense day:

    a. You will read your paper aloud.

    b. Then the group will try to find your position.

    c. You will be asked to describe how you organized your paper.

    d. You will respond to a variety of questions about your position, your examples, your mechanics, as well as the book.

    e. The group will decide on a consensus grade or evaluation at the end of the discussion.

Lesson 33
Chunking a Decade Artifact

Goal

Understanding how literature relates to oneself and to the culture, as preparation for writing the bestseller artifact paper.

Materials

A decade short story. Suggestion: Berton Roueche's "Phone Call" (1962). If small-group chunking is chosen for the lesson, the story should be marked into segments with arrows indicating where the reading of each segment begins and ends.

Assignment

1. The students should know their due date for their artifact paper on bestsellers.

2. The instructor has the option of completing this lesson in class or extending it one or more days.

Procedure

Options: Reading, discussion, and writing.

1. The entire story and assignment can be done in class. The instructor activates prior knowledge by dealing with questions that are addressed in the story, for example, in "Phone Call." Q: "Have you ever had car trouble? What happened?" Q: "Have you ever been in a situation when you were threatened with physical assault? What happened? How did you get out of it?"

Then announce the title of the story, asking the students to freewrite what they think the story is going to be about. Then read the rest of the story in chunks. After each chunk, the students freewrite and share their responses as to what that segment of the story made them feel, as well as anything else that might relate to the decade. Before the last chunk, ask the students to predict the ending. Finally, the students write and share a final meaning of this artifact.

2. The lesson can be extended by an assigned writing. The instructor uses the same reading and questioning approach, but does not read the

final chunk or ending. Instead, the students are asked to write an ending and share their endings. The writing may begin in class and may be shared the next day. Or the students may write their own story based on their own experience, all suggested by this decade artifact, to be shared later.

3. Small groups can engage in chunking the artifact. The instructor distributes story copies with marked "chunks," along with the following handout on small-group directions.

Small Group: Chunking an Artifact

Small-Group Directions: A Short Story as Artifact

Form circles of five or six students. Everyone should have writing paper. Pick a chair to lead the group and a recorder to report to the class.

1. The chair should begin by asking the group to write about what the title of the story suggests. What do they think the story is going to be about? Share your answers.

2. Then the chair calls on individual students to read the marked passages aloud and briefly summarize what is happening—the people and the plot. Then everyone writes. The students can either write questions about the passage and share them with the group. Or they can write answers to *one* of the following questions and share the answer with the group: (a) How does the passage make you feel? (b) What details stand out the most? (c) Does the passage remind you of any experiences you've had? (d) What might happen next?

3. Write one important meaning of the story in terms of human experience or the American decade. Then the group should either select one student's response to share with the class. Or the group should work together to form a consensus meaning. The secretary-recorder should read that consensus meaning to the class.

Lessons 34–36 Choices

Goal

Finish reading bestsellers in preparation for position papers and defense day, as well as conferring with students about term papers.

Assignment

Position papers are due _____ . Remember that you will have to photocopy four papers for the two (or more) defense days.

Materials

1. Copies of bestsellers.

2. Handout 16: "Evaluating Position Papers for Defense Day."

3. Handout 17: "A Collaborative Student Position Paper."

Procedure

1. Students should be reading their bestsellers and preparing for their position papers. Remind them of the due dates. Distribute handouts. Note that all four students will be evaluated by the same procedure.

2. During these lessons, call for the term project proposals and hold conferences with students. The conferences may also be held when student and instructor have matching free time outside of class.

3. Suggestions for individual conferences with students:

    a. Make sure that all students have different projects—or different approaches to the same general topic.

    b. Work with the students on narrowing.

    c. If possible, work together on a tentative outline to the project.

    d. Suggest what the next step of the research might be.

    e. Encourage the students to have brief follow-up conferences on their progress.

    f. If some students foresee major changes, ask them to make another proposal.

    g. Make notes of key ideas and concerns of the conference for the students to take with them.

Lessons 37–39
Defense Days

Goal

Understanding that bestsellers are cultural artifacts that transmit and reinforce values, through defense day small groups.

Materials

1. Class copies of the bestsellers.

2. Handout 16: extra defense day evaluation sheets.

3. Photocopies of the four (or more) position papers for the defense days.

Procedure

1. Students should be reminded of their small-group defense days, and they should receive photocopies of the two papers that they will be reading, evaluating, and annotating. Remind the students to review the evaluation sheet and bring it to their group sessions.

2. When groups are not in session, the students can be working on their projects. Or you may wish to have only two groups, with one group observing the other group for that day.

3. Defense day procedure:

    a. Make sure that all students have copies of the two position papers, as well as evaluation vehicles (Handout 16). Remind the students that each paper will take half the period to evaluate.

    b. Ask the first writer to read his or her paper aloud.

    c. Call on a student to state the position. Repeat the statement until the student is satisfied. Then ask other students if they agree. If basic consensus is there but needs to be worded differently, try to frame a consensus position agreeable to the group. If the group finds no clear consensus, repeat that as well. Don't let the writer talk until consensus, or the lack of it, is reached!

    d. Then ask the writer, "How are we doing? Did anybody have what you wanted?" Let the writer expand on this.

e. Next ask the writer to go page by page, describing how the organization and support were developed.

f. Then open the discussion broadly: "What do you think? What do you like about this paper? Do you have any questions? Do you see anything that gave you trouble, that might be improved?"

g. Finally, go page by page, noting any mechanical problems.

h. Then go back to the first responder and ask for an evaluation grade based on the three points of the evaluation sheet, as well as such things as originality. Then call on one or more students to do the same before making a roll call grading by the rest of the students. Take notes on the grades and announce the average. Write this grade on the paper.

i. Repeat this procedure with the second writer. Distribute all of the position papers at the end of the period.

Evaluating Position Papers for Defense Day

Handout
16

Clarity of Position _____

1. Does the paper pursue one position?

2. Does this position clearly reveal some insight into American culture or the decade or both?

3. Can you state this position? If so, write it below:

Organization and Support _____

1. Is the position clear because it is logical?

2. Is it clear because it is supported by concrete material such as direct references and quotations?

3. Does the paper suffer from irrelevancies or overemphasis of a minor point?

4. Is the paper clear because it pursues an obvious position, if not a minor one? Consider whether the position is original and challenging.

5. Is there coherence in the paper: transitions between sentences and paragraphs to enhance the organization?

6. Is the position supported by proper language; for example, a humorous position using humorous images and words?

7. Are the introduction and conclusion effective in clarifying the position?

Mechanics _____

1. Is the reader distracted from the paper's position by many proofreading errors? Are there more than ten basic mechanical errors?

2. Is the paper smooth reading? What about awkward sentences, imprecise or redundant choices?

Teaching the Sixties by Brooke Workman. © 1992 NCTE. Copied by permission.

A Collaborative Student Position Paper: Bestsellers as Artifacts

Black Like Me: A New Way of Seeing America

The 1960s was a critical time in American history, a time of enormous change. Lifestyles were changing as fast as the new technology. Yet these changes did not happen all at once. For example, at the beginning of the decade, the barriers of racial prejudice were still there, especially in the South. And a book called *Black Like Me* showed just how bad things were.

Its author, John Howard Griffin, was out to find what it was like to be a black man in the South—or rather a white man who managed to disguise himself as one. As he migrated into "The Black World" of New Orleans, Louisiana, and Mississippi, he couldn't understand how his race, the white race, could be so different. Soon he began to think and to see in a new way. Even his memories of his wife and children were changed.

As he began to journey to the South, Griffin developed a new awareness of prejudice. In New Orleans, for example, he was afraid that people who knew him when he was white would recognize him and be unhappy with his disguise. However, this did not happen. When he did reveal his secret, such as to a black shoeshine man, he was encouraged and given advice on how to survive.

If anything, he found that whites didn't pay much attention to blacks, though one white lady on a bus accused him of being rude by staring at her. It just seemed like whites didn't know blacks were there! He was invisible.

In Mississippi, things were different, more threatening. There, he couldn't use the same restaurants or restrooms as whites. Blacks had to tell him who to talk to and where to go—and even who to hang around with.

On one bus trip, Griffin discovered a bus driver who would not let blacks off the bus to use the restroom, even though he had already let the whites off. Griffin also found that it was actually dangerous to go out at night for fear that a car would drive down the street and throw something at him. In fact, this actually happened to him, but luckily he wasn't injured.

John Howard Griffin gathered experience that ranged from near invisibility in New Orleans to outward hostility in Mississippi—all because of the color on his white skin. While some people would talk to him, everywhere he had to be careful about what to say and where to eat, to stand, to walk, to sit, to look. Oddly enough, he found that his allies were people who had the same color on their skin. And so he was a changed man in the 1960s.

Then he went home and wrote his story, the first story of its kind. Some readers may have accused him of never really understanding what it means to be a Black American because he could always escape and remove his disguise. However, we believe that his bravery and his book helped change America. *Black Like Me* became part of the great Civil Rights movement. John Howard Griffin's best seller opened the eyes of many Americans as they entered the critical decade of the 1960s.

Teaching the Sixties by Brooke Workman. © 1992 NCTE. Copied by permission.

Lesson 40
Self-Evaluation

Goal

Self-evaluation by students, as well as some commentary about the course.

Materials

1. Handout 18: "Self-Evaluation."
2. Handout 19: "Folder Record—First Period Evaluations."

Procedure

1. Even though the first grading period may not be over, or the course at midpoint, this may be a good time for self-evaluation. In fact, with the usual interruptions of class schedule in an average high school, this may be the midpoint of the course. In any case, this will be a good time to stop, to evaluate the students and to consider the students' self-evaluations. Also, doing the evaluations now will not interrupt the next section on architecture and painting.

2. Using the student folders with teacher and observer evaluations and comments, as well as Handout 18 on self-evaluation (one to each student), the students should spend this period writing their self-evaluations and final grade that corresponds with the school's grading system. They should review each item on the handout; the instructor should remind them of each assigned responsibility.

3. The self-evaluation is an important factor in determining the course grade. If the instructor disagrees with a student's self-evaluation, a conference should be held immediately for a couple of reasons: (a) The instructor may feel that the student grade is too low or too high. (b) The conference will be an in-depth discussion of the grade and perhaps a time for bargaining. Past experience indicates that few problems arise from the self-evaluation and the conference system, probably because it is a positive system of evaluation, useful to everyone concerned.

4. Note: The folder record (Handout 19) offers space for write-in assignments and evaluations, such as alternate suggestions in the lessons or other assignments given by the instructor.

Self-Evaluation

Directions

Below is an outline of various points to consider in arriving at your grade for the first period. Go through each point and describe in writing your performance. Also note the marks and comments made by the instructor and observers in your folder. You might even grade yourself on each section in order to arrive at your final grade.

Remember

If you have not completed the assignments or if you were late, and if you have any unexcused absences, you should not expect or ask for high evaluations.

I. Requirements

1. Values Analysis 1
2. Values Analysis 2
3. Artifact Day Presentation
4. Identification: Decade Terms
5. Activity Committee Work: Handbook, Bulletin Board, Artifacts, TV
6. Small Group: History
7. Oral History, Genealogy, Date Research: Paper, Chart, Presentation
8. Decade Film Analysis
9. Bestsellers: Position Paper
10. Term Project Proposal

II. Your Best Work

Describe the assignment that is your best work. Why is it your best work? What did you learn?

III. Points for Instructor to Consider

1. Attendance (any unexcused absences?)
2. Prior Knowledge of Materials
3. Outside Preparation (What do you feel that the instructor should know about your work?)

4. Personal Factors Affecting Performance (What do you feel might have hurt your work, such as sickness, part-time jobs, personal problems, workload in other course?)

5. Problems Relating to the Instructor (Do you feel that the instructor has been unfair to you?)

IV. Grade or Evaluation: _____

Folder Record—First Period Evaluations by Instructor and Observers

Handout **19**

1. **Values Analysis 1: Top Ten TV**

    _____ Comments:

2. **Values Analysis 2: Dominant Values**

    _____ Comments:

3. **Artifact Day: Presentation**

    _____ Comments:

4. **Identification: History Terms**

    _____ Comments:

5. **Activity Committee: Handbook, Bulletin Board, Artifacts, TV**

    _____ Comments:

6. **Small Group: History**

    _____ Comments:

7. **Oral History, Date Research, Genealogy**

    _____ Comments:

8. **Decade Film Analysis**

_____ Comments:

9. **Bestsellers: Position Paper**

_____ Comments:

10. **Term Project Proposal**

_____ Comments:

11. _____

_____ Comments:

12. _____

_____ Comments:

Lessons 41–55
Architecture and Paintings
as Artifacts

[T]he great variety in the subject matter of humanities instruction facilitates an understanding of cultural diversity.

The English Coalition: Democracy through Language (85)

Lesson 41
Architecture as Artifact

Goal

Orientation to the American Humanities concept that a building is an artifact and reveals values of a culture.

Materials

1. Two handouts: "Architecture as Artifact" (Handout 20) and "Architecture—Values Analysis" (Handout 21).

2. School-made slides of local architecture, for example, front and rear orientations of houses of the decades 1890 to 1970; dream houses of the decades. Encourage the students to take slide photographs of local buildings, including the two that they compare.

3. For descriptions of dream houses, you may find it helpful to refer to Mary Mix Foley's *The American House,* especially the section on "America's Dream House," pages 220–221.

Procedure

1. During the next few lessons, encourage the students in their research, even to the point of developing weekend gatherings to study and learn about local resources, especially libraries that have magazines on permanent reserve or microfilm facilities.

   You may wish to devote class time to reviewing research techniques:

   a. "The Magic Box": Bring a research box—and develop the idea of centralizing research. Ask the students to guess what is in the box. Then open it and gradually reveal its contents—a stylebook or sheet on bibliography and footnotes, sample note cards, a *Roget Thesaurus,* a spelling dictionary, a sample term paper. Encourage the students to keep materials in one place so that they will remember where they are.

   b. Distribute any school handouts on research, such as a term paper stylesheet. Devote time to using the *Reader's Guide,* as well as suggestions for note-taking, building a bibliography, being careful about plagiarism.

2. The students should have reached step 5 of the Ten Steps to a Successful Project (see Lesson 26). Note: The instructor should keep

this ten-step list on the chalkboard for the remainder of the course, noting the progressive steps and due dates. Announce the due date for the sentence outline. Again remind students that *this is not the final outline*, which will appear with their term papers *after* they have completed the final draft. This sentence outline is simply a tool for the second conference, a way of mutual understanding of what the students are thinking, of where the research is taking them. Suggestion: Provide the students with a copy of a sample sentence outline.

3. Then shift to a values discussion. Ask the students how much of a person's time, if not income, is involved with buildings—living and working in them, paying rent and making house payments. Ask them if they know the date and style of their school. Then poll the students on how many have taken a course where architecture has been discussed and taught. Can they name a famous American architect? Why is so little time spent on architecture if it is so important?

4. Distribute Handouts 20 and 21, noting the written assignment on local architecture, including the option of partner collaboration. Ask the students to review the handouts for the next lessons.

5. Complete the discussion with one or more of the following topics:

    a. Inventory the class on the date or decade of their homes. If they do not know, how can they find out? Where can they find a map of their community? Note: Copies of recent town and city maps may be purchased at the city hall.

       Describe the concentric circle theory of dating buildings. Using the chalkboard or an overhead with a photocopy of a community map, start with the oldest standing buildings, which are usually near the center of the community, and then draw concentric circles that represent decades, arriving at the present. Note the 1960s, too.

    b. Old versus new homes. Why do some people prefer either old or new buildings? A chalkboard list of contrasting values will convey the concept of a house as part of people's values. One should note that old styles such as colonial are still being used in new homes.

    c. How can we date a building? How can we *see* immediate value differences between past and present? Show slides of local nineteenth century buildings, as well as houses with and without front porches. Show the rear orientation of these houses as well. Speculate on what orientation means. (See essay on architecture that follow.)

    d. Ask a final question: What is American architecture? Ask the students if they have ever heard of Frank Lloyd Wright.

Additional and Alternative Suggestion: The Learning Log

1. Architecture as artifact is a popular subject with students and can be extended, especially through learning log writing and oral response. An example follows.

> *Day 1:* "Architecture as Artifact" (Lesson 41). Assign: "From Porch to Patio" (text follows Lesson 43). Summarize the important concepts of the essay in learning log entry 1 and be prepared to share it on day 2.

> *Day 2:* Sharing of learning log 1 entries. Review dream houses, with slides. Discussion of handouts with entries on "eclecticism," using slides. Assign learning log entry 2. Reflect on eclectic buildings of your community. What do they say about American values? How do you feel about them?

> *Day 3:* Sharing of learning log 2 entries. Discussion of "organic architecture" topic with handouts, with slides or a film on Frank Lloyd Wright (see Bibliography). Assign learning log entry 3: What does the film reveal about the meaning of "organic"? Is organic architecture truly American? Do you prefer eclectic or organic? Explain.

> *Day 4:* Sharing of learning log 3 entries. Review handouts on the topic of "international architecture," with slides. What would the eclectic or organic architects say about this architecture? Is this more American than organic? Learning log entry 4: Would you prefer to have an international house or an organic one? Explain.

> *Day 5:* Sharing of learning log 4 entries. Assign a poem about a famous American building, especially one of the 1960s. Using slides or a film, review famous American buildings, such as the late 1950s–early 1960s St. Louis Arch by Eero Saarinen. (The video "Monument to the Dream: The Construction of the Arch" is available from the St. Louis Arch, Jefferson National Expansion Historical Society, St. Louis, Missouri.)

> *Day 6:* Sharing poems. Architecture as Artifact paper is due. Final in-class learning log entry: What did I learn in this section on architecture? Turn in learning log.

2. Any one of the above lessons or ideas may be used as a substitute for Lessons 41–43.

3. *Day 7* (alternate or addition): Ask the students to do an in-class drawing of what a model school—inside and out—should look like. Have them share their drawings and theories, especially in terms of values and education.

Lesson 42
Architecture as Artifact

Goal

Familiarization with eclectic and organic architecture, especially with Frank Lloyd Wright, an American who wanted to develop an American architecture.

Materials

1. Handout 22: "Written Assignment—Architecture as Artifact."

2. Slides of local eclectic buildings, as well as buildings by Louis Sullivan and Wright. School-prepared slides on famous Washington, D.C., eclectic buildings.

3. Option: Recordings of popular 1960s songs such as Simon and Garfunkel's "So Long, Frank Lloyd Wright" and Pete Seeger's "Little Boxes."

Assignment

Short paper: Architecture as Artifact. Note that two partners may collaborate on the research and writing of this paper.

Procedure

1. Review the concept that a building is an artifact and reveals values. Refer to the handout and to the word *eclectic*. Note the material on eclecticism in the handout.

2. Show community slides of eclectic buildings, especially familiar landmarks such as school and community buildings. Show the Washington, D.C., slides to reinforce the idea that early America copied architecture from great civilizations such as Greece and Rome.

3. Ask the students the following questions: (a) What does it mean that a building must *say* what it *does?* Does a local school building look as if it were made for education, or does it resemble something else, such as a factory for mass production or a business? (b) What does it mean when an architect says that our architecture must be American?

4. Refer to the handout discussion of organic architecture. Note the names of Sullivan and Wright. Ask if anyone has ever seen a Sullivan

or Wright building, such as those in Illinois (especially Chicago), Wisconsin, Pennsylvania, New York, or California. Refer to the names of the buildings at the bottom of the handout.

5. Show school-prepared or commercial slides of Wright and Sullivan buildings and skyscrapers. Suggestions:

    a. Wright: Taliesin East and West, Guggenheim Museum, the Robie House in Chicago (1909), Falling Water near Bear Run, Pennsylvania, or the Johnson Wax factory at Racine, Wisconsin.

    b. Sullivan: the Carson, Pirie, Scott department store in Chicago, an early skyscraper.

6. Describe Wright's battle to establish what he felt was truly Amerian architecture, which was recognized by the 1960s musicians Simon and Garfunkel. During Lesson 43, you may wish to show a film on Wright, who died in 1959, leaving his legacy to the sixties.

Additional Suggestions

1. If any Wright or Sullivan buildings are in or near your community, the class should consider a field trip.

2. Develop an architecture bulletin board, using a copy of a city map. Ask students to develop a visual display of local architecture by bringing photographs of their homes or buildings that interest them—and locating them on the map.

Handout **20**

Architecture as Artifact

I. Criticism of American Architecture

Criticism began as early as the 1920s with the attacks on the superficiality of eclecticism.

II. Eclecticism

1. Borrowing from established systems of architecture, often from Europe. Even today, people build buildings in the styles mentioned in a 1926 book on the American "modern" home: (a) Dutch Colonial, (b) Early American, (c) New England Colonial, (d) Southern Colonial, (e) English Tudor, (f) English Georgian, (g) Italian Villa, (h) Spanish home.

2. Early skyscrapers had Gothic features from the cathedrals of the Middle Ages.

3. No concern for local climate or terrain or history of the family or country, or for people's needs.

III. Organic Architecture (Functionalism)

This new (in the 1920s) and very American architecture took its inspiration from Louis Sullivan ("Form follows function") and his student Frank Lloyd Wright, who developed it until his death at the end of the 1950s. Organic architecture opposed eclecticism, seeking buildings which had a form that grew out of the needs of Americans, their ideals and landscape. Wright's "prairie house" was a home for the Midwest. An example is Taliesin at Spring Green, Wisconsin, which was rebuilt in the 1920s. Beginning in the 1930s, Wright built organic houses such as Falling Water at Bear Run, Pennsylvania; organic factories such as the Johnson Wax factory in Racine, Wisconsin; and organic art museums such as the 1950s Guggenheim Museum in New York City.

IV. International Style

In Europe in the 1930s, especially in France, Germany, and Finland, a style of architecture developed, stressing buildings that were symbolic of industrial society, placing emphasis on more glass, more horizontals, rounded corners, and reinforced concrete. Leaders of this international style were Walter Gropius of Germany, Mies van der Rohe of Germany, Eliel Saarinen of Finland, and Le Corbusier of France. All had their impact on America. Many of these architects came to the fertile soil of industry and technology, the United States of America. While some critics found the international style to be coldly economical and machinelike, it became very popular in the 1950s and 1960s. Later, this style was modified into what is sometimes called "contemporary architecture."

V. Buildings of Interest

1. 1920s: Wright's Taliesin (1914–25), Tokyo's Imperial Hotel (1916–22), Richard Neutra's Lovell House (1929), Los Angeles.

2. 1930s: Wright's Taliesin West (1938–59) near Phoenix, Johnson Wax Building (1936–39), Falling Water (1936), Empire State Building (1930–31) in New York City.

3. 1945–60: Wright's Guggenheim Museum (1959), Mies van der Rohe's New York and Chicago houses and buildings such as the 1958 Seagram Building in New York City.

4. 1960s: U.S. Pavilion at Montreal (1967) by Buckminster Fuller, CBS Building (1962–64) in New York City, and the St. Louis Gateway Arch (completed in 1966) by Eero Saarinen.

Architecture—Values Analysis

Style	Values
Style	**Values**
1. Eclectic: imitation; blending of previous styles, often from Europe, e.g., Gothic towers on Chicago Tribune Building (1920s).	External conformity, orientation to the past, belief that culture comes from abroad.
2. Organic: Louis Sullivan (1856–1924) and Frank Lloyd Wright (1869–1959). (a) "Form follows function." (b) The structure is designed for people who will live in it. (c) The structure conforms to its site, to the landscape. (d) The structure is made from the materials of the landscape.	Freedom and individuality. An attempt to have a truly American architecture based on our concept of choice and, perhaps, on our love of nature. Note: See song lyrics to "So Long, Frank Lloyd Wright," by Simon and Garfunkel.
3. Public or government, especially 1930s projects, e.g., schools, dams, government buildings, park buildings, bridges built by WPA, PWA, CCC; theaters.	External conformity (eclectic), nationalism and patriotism, efficiency and practicality. Architecture functional to the nation, representative of history, symbolic of a dynamic society.
4. Skyscrapers: 1920s to 1960s, especially Empire State Building, CBS, Rockefeller Center, Seagram Building, St. Louis Arch.	Progress, science and technology, architecture as symbol of a dynamic culture.
5. International style: Eliel and Eero Saarinen, Walter Gropius, Mies van der Rohe, Richard Neutra, Le Corbusier, Philip Johnson.	Progress, science and technology, efficiency; buildings as machines; symbols of a dynamic, mechanized society, though often cold and impersonal. Note: Furniture for these buildings was made of tubular steel and other man-made materials.

6. Buckminster Fuller (1895–1983), geodesic dome. A house as a "living machine." Plan for a dome covering Manhattan; tension more important than compression; strong appeal to the young in the 1960s.

Progress means mobility: since Americans are mobile, so must their buildings be. Technology is the salvation of our people; reform the environment, not humans. "Trees have roots; men have legs."

Written Assignment—Architecture as Artifact

Compare two buildings of the same order (schools, houses, public buildings), one from the 1960s and one from the present (within the past ten years) or from 1890 to 1955. Write at least a one-page analysis of the two buildings, covering the following points:

1. Note the similarities and/or differences between the two.
2. Develop a theory as to what the buildings mean as artifacts.
3. Use architectural terms such as *eclectic, organic, international.*

Points to Consider

Naturally you are not an architect. Perhaps you have never even looked closely at the buildings around you. Have you thought of buildings as representatives of cultural values? Have you thought about what people—such as your parents—want in a home or public building? Have you closely examined parts of a building: doors, windows, the size and shape, the decoration, the materials, the front and the back, the use of line and color, the inside and the outside?

How do you feel as you look at the building? Indifferent? Proud? Where does your eye go as you look at the building? Does the form remind you of its function? For example, does a school look like a place where learning occurs? Does the building fit its site? Does the building have symbolic significance? For example, does it remind you of a machine? a temple? Is it based on a concept of efficiency? Is it imitative of styles of architecture from early history? Is it American?

Specifics

1. *The site:* Does the building relate to the site, the landscape?

2. *The function:* Is the building designed to do what it is supposed to do? Is it made for the people who will use it?

3. *The materials:* Do the materials relate to the site, and perhaps come from the local environment?

4. *The period:* Does the building seem to be an integral part of the American time period, or is it a borrowing from another time and place?

Suggestion: Study the model student paper (Handout 23).

Lesson 43
Architecture as Artifact

Goal

Reinforcement of the idea that a building is an artifact and that some Americans, such as Frank Lloyd Wright and Buckminster Fuller, have tried to establish an American architecture, organic and functional. Orientation to international architecture. Develop contrast of eclectic and organic to international.

Materials

1. School-prepared slides on eclectic architecture.

2. Handout 23: "Student Paper: Architecture as Artifact."

3. (Optional) Copies of the article "From Porch to Patio," which follows this lesson. (To copy and distribute this handout for your students, contact: Educational Permissions, Copyright Clearance Center, 27 Congress St., Salem, MA 01970; (508) 744-3350.)

Procedure

1. Review the previous lessons on buildings as artifacts, on eclectic architecture versus the organic of Sullivan and Wright, who wished to develop an American architecture that matched the values of individuality and freedom.

2. Distribute the handout of a student's paper on this assignment.

3. Show slides of international architecture, as well as review the parts of Handouts 20 and 21 on this style. Be sure to include slides of buildings by Richard Neutra, Philip Johnson, Eero Saarinen, and Buckminster Fuller.

4. Since Saarinen's St. Louis Arch and Fuller's geodesic dome are famous 1960s structures, you may wish to focus on their appeal, their values. For information on Fuller, see Alden Hatch's *Buckminster Fuller: At Home in the Universe* (1974). Why would the 1960s be so excited by the arch and the dome?

5. Seek both oral and written responses to these architects and buildings. Ask for freewrites and shared responses to international buildings, as well as to the students' preference—eclectic, organic, or international.

Additional or Alternative Suggestions

1. Show a film on architecture, on a specific architect such as Frank Lloyd Wright. (See Bibliography.)

2. A teacher or an architect from the community should be invited to discuss architecture as artifact, as well as his or her feelings about American architecture and specific architects.

FROM PORCH TO PATIO

by Richard H. Thomas

Two assumptions are basic to understanding the role of architecture in our lives: first, domestic dwellings in their construction and design reflect the prevailing cultural notions of what a *home* should be (the reflection of what the owner sees as being essential to his style of life); second, a house is not only a shelter, but it may be viewed also as a statement of the way personal and social life is organized.

The century between 1860 and 1960 saw many changes in technology, values, population, land use, and the structure of social and political institutions. These changes were often rather rapid and accompanied by new tensions between the desire for privacy and the need to be public enough to enjoy the benefits of community life. The home architecture of what can be termed the "gentry" (the social and economic upper class who were the architectural style leaders as well as the business and often the intellectual elite) demonstrated some of these changing notions of privacy and community. There is no question that the other socioeconomic classes attempted to imitate the lead of the gentry and designed their homes with features that resembled the houses of their "betters" (to use the nineteenth-century term).

It is enlightening to look at one particular feature of architectural design: the porch. The gradual movement of the porch from the front of the house to the back (where it became the modern patio) illustrates the importance of new technology in home building and tells us a great deal about the social meaning of homes. Focusing just on the porch leaves out many important elements of the home, such as the arrangement of rooms within the structure or the evolution of the nineteenth-century parlor into the modern den. However, a concentrated look at the porch enables us to see how the use of new materials and an increasing desire for privacy modified not only the artistic design of the house, but suggested new forms of social relations with one's

The porch of the M. Heisey residence in Anamosa, Iowa was relatively small, but clearly the center of much social activity (from Andreas Atlas, 1875).

Originally published as Richard H. Thomas, "From Porch to Patio," *Palimpsest* 56 (July/August 1975): 120–127. Copyright 1975 State Historical Society of Iowa. Used here by permission of the publisher.

Brucemoor, an elegant gentry house, now owned by Mrs. Howard Hall of Cedar Rapids.

neighbors. This in turn may illustrate shifting ideas about what is meant by a sense of community or belonging to a particular place.

A central social development during the century between 1860 and 1960 was the compression of time and distance, accelerating the tempo of life. In the late nineteenth century, most of the gentry class built homes on large lots, usually facing the street. The homes were designed to be viewed from a horse-drawn buggy as it approached and passed at a slow pace, thus letting the viewer see and appreciate the entire home including its many points of interest and intricate designs. Many of these homes today are crowded by other structures, and when the passerby travels at an average speed of 25 miles per hour, viewing time is reduced to approximately six to ten seconds. We often fail to appreciate some of the grandeur of these homes because of the speed at which we are accustomed to traveling and the congestion of other structures. The porch is especially important in this context of speed. In an earlier day the viewer riding in a carriage

A marvelous porch, which extended across the entire front of the house, and which could accommodate the entire family, plus visitors. Note the low fence between sidewalk and yard.

or the citizen walking past the house saw the building for a long time and was well aware of the presence or absence of the residents on the porch.

The city or country porch presented opportunities for social intercourse at several levels. When a family member was on the porch it was possible to exchange a wave or a trivial greeting with those passing by. On the other hand, it was also possible to invite the passerby to stop and come up onto the porch for extended conversation. The person on the porch was very much in control of this interaction, as the porch was seen as an extension of the living quarters of the family. Often, a hedge or fence separated the porch from the street or board sidewalk, providing a physical barrier for privacy, yet low enough to permit conversation. The porch served many important social functions in addition to advertising the availability of its inhabitants. A well-shaded porch provided a cool place in the heat of the day for the women to enjoy a rest from household chores. They could exchange gossip or share problems without having to arrange a "neighborhood coffee" or a "bridge party." The porch also provided a courting place within earshot of protective parents. A boy and a girl could be close on a porch swing, yet still observed, and many a proposal of marriage was made on a porch swing. Older persons derived great pleasure from sitting on the porch, watching the world go by, or seeing the neighborhood children at play. The gentry homes were intentionally designed to provide a place for entertainment, and a summer porch was often the location of such gatherings.

The humblest of homes could not do without some form of a porch. It was a pervasive architectural form which disappeared slowly. Part of the resistance toward abandoning the porch as an essential part of the home can be attributed to the primary group relationships that permeated both the large and small communities. It was important to know one's neighbors and be known by them. The porch was a platform from which to observe the activities of others. It also facilitated and symbolized a set of social relationships and the strong bond of community feeling which people during the nineteenth century supposed was the way God intended life to be lived.

Slowly, technology and changes both in taste and social structure began to alter the form and the meaning of the porch. By the turn of the century a well established sash and door industry, new building materials, and innovative construction techniques granted home builders an even greater variety of porch styles from which to select. Labor was still cheaper than material. The gentry maintained their social and economic position, constructing homes much along the lines of the previous 30 years. Those with power and wealth seemed unafraid to let others know their status by constructing large and elaborate homes, but taste had begun to change. A few years before the dawn of the century Louis Sullivan, Frank Lloyd Wright, and others were searching for a new architecture which would

The women of the household relax on the porch of the Baptist parsonage in Vinton, Iowa. The spacious lawn and upper porch give an air of relaxed elegance to this example of the "porch" society.

A porch extending around two sides of the house at the C. E. Gillette home in Mt. Vernon, Iowa.

become distinctly American. Both men found patrons among the Iowa gentry for commercial as well as domestic buildings. The influence of Wright's Prairie School of design is most evident in a series of structures in the Mason City area. Most of Iowa's gentry, however, preferred to modify the styles of the late nineteenth century rather than adopt the avant-garde notions of Frank Lloyd Wright.

Most Iowans were not of the gentry class and could not afford the opulent displays of wealth prevalent among the social aristocracy. Many, however, began to build bungalows or single-story dwellings which were made economically feasible by the increasing mechanization of the millwork industry. Yet, a large proportion of these

modest structures continued the tradition of some form of the porch.

By the 1920s, signs of a new architectural style were evident. The slow breakdown of many of the values of the late nineteenth century continued, and the gentry classes lost power. This was accompanied by massive technological changes symbolized by electricity and the internal combustion engine. The two decades of social and economic change which followed World War I created markets for small, single-family dwellings. Population in rural areas continued to shift toward the cities, and with the coming of the industrial expansion of World War II, pressing needs for low-cost housing brought the techniques of mass produc-

Backyard patios near Cedar Rapids.

tion into the housing industry as never before. Federal subsidies for housing further stimulated the building boom. The population explosion following World War II and a spiraling economic cycle gave added thrust to home construction. At the edge of cities, planned and unplanned communities sprang up without the homes or the influence of the once powerful and respected gentry class who in an earlier day had set the example of the most desirable homes and fixed the patterns of social relations.

The demand for new housing, the presence of a large number of trained architects, and vast subsidies for middle-class housing, together with new financial resources all contributed to a massive building boom. In the new suburbia land was costly, labor more expensive than any of the new materials available to contractors, and architects were often the hirelings of large development corporations whose profits rested heavily on standardized construction and prefabrication. These new communities were frequently "bedroom cities" which lacked established social structures and the ingredients of community building prevalent in the older towns and villages. Many suburbanites were refugees from the city, seeking a style of single-family dwelling which would maintain the privacy afforded by the anonymity of urban culture.

Mass production, however, left little room for innovation or creation. Young

The modern style is exemplified by the Len Walworth residence in Burlington (courtesy of Mc-Connell, Steveley, & Anderson Architects, Cedar Rapids, Iowa).

persons in the planned communities wanted to make their homes distinguishable from the same models down the street, and they wanted also to make their homes private. Perhaps the most frequently used device in the search for uniqueness and privacy was the backyard patio. In communities with a high rate of mobility, one did not often want to know his neighbor. The constant turn-over of neighbors worked against the long-term relationships which are essential to a sense of belonging. The patio, walled on one, two, or three sides, was a barrier for privacy and a means of self-expression.

The patio was an extension of the house, but far less public than the porch. It was easy to greet a stranger from the porch but exceedingly difficult to do so from the backyard patio. While the porch was designed in an era of slow movement, the patio is part of a world which places a premium on speed and ease of access. The father of a nineteenth-century family might stop on the porch on his way into the house, but the suburban man wishes to enter the house as rapidly as possible to accept the shelter that the house provides from the mass of people he may deal with all day.

In this transition from porch to patio there is an irony. Nineteenth-century families were expected to be public and fought to achieve their privacy. Part of the sense of community that often characterized the nineteenth-century village resulted from the forms of social interaction that the porch facilitated. Twentieth-century man has achieved the sense of privacy in his patio, but in doing so he has lost part of his public nature which is essential to strong attachments and a deep sense of belonging or feelings of community. Whether the patio is surrounded by walls or left open, it usually remains in the rear of the house, providing privacy but creating a barrier to informal social contacts once provided by the porch. In the hurried flight from commuter vehicle to the sanctuary of the home there is no time or real desire for informal contacts without which a sense of belonging is difficult to establish and maintain. Today social forms revolve around the car and the ability to maintain friendships over a wide geographic area. The modern home has moved the "car-barn" into the house itself. Today's home embraces the car, providing it almost as much shelter as the family. The carriage house of the past century was usually on the back of the lot, and while the horse was in some sense a part of the family, it did not occupy the living space as does the car and the garage of today. Another irony here is that the car has both freed us and enslaved us.

The preoccupation of the commuter as he speeds through suburbia is how to pick out of the hundreds of similar models the single dwelling that is indeed *his* home. He lives in a world that gives only a three second view of houses as he looks from his car window. He finds himself in a sterile environment where domestic architectural creativity is restricted by very high building costs. Thus he takes to the "do-it-yourself" skills involving a small saw, paint, and wallpaper.

It should be noted that now as in the past many architects continue to find patrons among the new upper-middle class who are anxious to separate themselves from the masses and want homes that reflect their status and taste. Doctors, lawyers, and rising business executives provide the capital for innovative structures. This new gentry seems committed to the privacy of the patio, and many of their homes reflect backyard areas open on three sides because the owners have purchased enough land to protect their privacy or view of the landscape.

The old cliche says, "A man's home is his castle." If this be true, the nineteenth-century porch was a drawbridge across which many passed in their daily lives. The modern patio is in many ways a closed courtyard that suggests that the king and his family are tired of the world and seek only the companionship of their immediate family or intimate peers. The tension between the need for privacy and the desire to belong to a community is still with us. The resolution of this seemingly ever-present conflict in needs and values is, and will be, mirrored in the design of whatever is called a house. □

Student Paper: Architecture as Artifact

Education and Architecture: A Lesson of Change

In the 1960s, the images and attitudes of this country's educational establishment changed markedly. Student activism and faculty liberalism created significant changes in the curriculum and structure of these schools, from the hippies at the universities to the high schools and grammar schools. The buildings were also changing during the Sixties, and these changes can reveal something about the country's changing educational outlook.

Iowa City's elementary school Horace Mann was built in 1917. It was built in eclectic, conservative style, with a rectangular shape and three floors. At the top of each wall, and at the corners at the top, are different types of decorations. There are doors in the middle of each wall which are decorated in various ways. One has a curved arch over the doors, with Corinthian designs at the top of fake pillars. Above another door is the name "Horace Mann" and the date, A.D. 1917, in Gothic-style print. Underneath the windows are designs of lines of protruding brick. In general, this building is a typical, eclectic, early twentieth-century school building.

Ernest Horn Elementary was built in 1968, and it is a very modern building of international style. It is one story, and it spreads over the ground in a mass of connected pentagons and rectangles. The roof is irregular and curved, similar to sand dunes. It is built out of brick, and there are few external adornments. There is one main entrance, which is shaded by a protruding overhang. On the front of this overhang, in simple letters, are the words "Ernest Horn Elementary." This school is more typical of the modern school buildings.

The contrast of these buildings shows not only the changing architectural taste of Iowa Citians between the two time periods, but also the changing educational values and attitudes.

One hint of these values is simply given by exploring the namesakes of these buildings. Horace Mann was a New Englander who was famous for encouraging public education. He was dissatisfied with the system he saw developing, and he studied the European school system to find answers. He looked back to Europe for a solution, rather than creating a new one. Ernest Horn, in contrast, was a University of Iowa professor, who became famous for his innovative methods for teaching spelling. He saw a problem and looked around himself for the answer—not back to Europe.

These two men, and the architecture of the schools named after them, clearly show the change in educational philosophy in America. In the time of Horace Mann Elementary, education was focused primarily on tradition. Classical education harkened back to our forefathers of Europe, and American education was not a separate ideology at all.

By the time of Ernest Horn, education had changed. Ernest Horn was considered a step forward in the style of education. Instead of the 1917 eclectic decoration and box-like classrooms for teaching children, it offered a one-floor, clean-line openness for learning with its moveable curtains that separated each room. Experimentation was encouraged in 1968, laying a foundation for new ways to see the world.

Ernest Horn Elementary and Horace Mann Elementary are quite different styles that reveal quite different educational philosophies of quite different decades. Architecture can often be used to measure the changes in attitudes of people who live and work with buildings—or, in this case, learn.

Lesson 44
Paintings as Artifacts

Goal

Orientation to the concept that paintings are artifacts of American culture.

Materials

1. A short film on painting and art. Suggestions: (a) *Art Appreciation: Enjoying Paintings,* (b) *Art of the Sixties.*

2. Handout 24: "Empathy Sheet."

3. Prepare a basic classroom art library with books and reproductions. Encourage students to bring their own contributions. Materials from the school and community libraries should begin the basic classroom library, although students may wish to do specific library research later.

Procedure

1. Review the concept of cultural artifacts: films, TV, bestsellers, buildings, and now paintings. Poll the class: How many art classes have the students taken since junior/middle school? How many are planning to take more before they graduate? Open a discussion about why so few students take art, although art is a lifetime value for educated Americans. Ask the students about art in their homes, in public buildings, at galleries. Ask the students about galleries—the closest to the school or community. Remind the college prep students that they will probably be taking a required core humanities class in college that will involve understanding art.

2. Assure the students that they will all succeed in the art section. They will have time in class to prepare with handouts, art books and magazines, and just one painting to teach to the class.

3. Distribute the empathy handout. The empathy sheet will give them a language for teaching their decade painting. Note: The empathy sheet closely relates to the first suggested film.

4. Show the film to begin the orientation to the visual experience of art as artifact. Share reactions to the film with an in-class freewrite.

5. Tell the students that tomorrow they will pick their art slides.

Additional Suggestion

To whet student interest: (1) Mix some 1960s art slides with others from other decades. See if the students can guess which are the 1960s works. (2) Take one decade painting and ask the students to do a freewrite response and then share their writings in small groups or with the class.

Lesson 45
The Armory Show

Goal

Understanding that the roots of modern American art date to the 1913 New York City Armory Show, where young artists of Europe and America rebelled against the Academy Art, which was imitative—an art tradition dating back to the Renaissance.

Materials

1. Slides of paintings by artists before the Armory Show, artists represented in the Armory Show, and decade artists. These slides can be prepared by the students, the instructor, the AV department, or borrowed from the art department.

2. Slide projector.

3. See "Teacher Notes: The Armory Show," following this lesson.

Procedure

1. Review the previous lesson on painting as artifact and a part of people's lives. Note that people today enjoy paintings that date from the Renaissance and earlier, as well as what is sometimes called "modern art." Note that modern art began as early as 1913 in America with the famous New York Armory Show. The artists of the 1960s seem especially attuned to this early rebellion because they delighted in bright colors and a new way of looking at shapes and lines.

2. Using the "Teacher Notes: The Armory Show," describe some of the background of the Armory Show. Try to convey the spirit and methods of the show. Note that many viewers were shocked by the new art, especially *Nude Descending a Staircase*, by the French painter Marcel Duchamp.

3. Develop the concept of the break with Academy Art:

    a. Begin by showing a slide of Leonardo da Vinci's *Mona Lisa*—the Academy standard of great art, especially in America. Then show a parody of this work by Marcel Duchamp.

    b. Continue to contrast Academy versus Armory, for example, da Vinci versus Munch, Gainsborough versus van Gogh, Gilbert Stuart versus Gauguin, Millet versus Picasso.

c. Ask the students to note the way they feel about the contrasts, the differences in shapes, lines, colors, as well as the imitation of reality, the subject matter. Ask the students why some people in 1913 (if not in the 1960s and today) might be shocked, angered, puzzled. Note that the modern artists could paint like Academy artists, but that they didn't want to. Dispel the idea that these artists could paint no better than untrained children. Try to find an early Academy painting by Picasso!

d. Then play a game without much discussion: Mix slides of artists in the Armory Show (the exact paintings are not necessary) with older Academy paintings. Ask the student to respond: "Armory" or "Academy." Suggestions:

Armory	Academy
Picasso	da Vinci
Matisse	Rembrandt
Kandinsky	David
Picabia	Botticelli
Léger	Van Dyck
Braque	Titian
Cézanne	Murillo
Rouault	Holbein
Gauguin	Michelangelo
Munch	Vermeer

e. Conclude with *Nude Descending a Staircase.* Note its slow-motion, Cubist effect. Refer to "Teacher Notes: The Armory Show." Ask the students why anyone would object to this work.

Additional Suggestion

If time permits, show all of the 1960s slides that have been chosen for empathy and artifact analysis. Tell the students they will be asked to teach one of these works.

Teacher Notes: The Armory Show

Handout

I. Background Facts

Exhibit of 1,300 works by 300 artists from Europe and America.

Official title: "New York City International Exhibition of Modern Art."

February 17, 1913, to March 15, 1913.

National Guard Armory on Lexington Avenue.

Later the show traveled to Boston and Chicago.

More than 62,000 people paid the $1 admission.

II. The First Modern Art Show

The Armory Show was the first of its kind in the United States, although the new art had been displayed in small shows such as those at the famous Alfred Stieglitz Photo-Success Gallery at 291 Fifth Avenue in New York. The directors belonged to the anti-Academy group; many belonged to what was called the American Ashcan School:

A. Arthur B. Davies, Walt Kuhn, Gutzon Borglum, Elmer MacRae, John Mowbray-Clarke, Jerome Myers, Jerome Taylor, Robert Henri.

B. They wished to show what they called modern art: from Goya, Ingres, and Delacroix through the Impressionists, Postimpressionists, Fauves, and Cubists. They were breaking with the tradition of the Old Masters.

C. The directors, especially Davies and Kuhn, went to great effort and expense to bring art from Europe, especially from Paris, to select it, ship it, and mount it properly in the Armory.

III. Reactions

A. Americans were puzzled, angered, and pleased. A *New York Tribune* critic, Royal Cortissoz: "Men, it was a bully show, but don't do it again." Walt Kuhn, as late as 1938: "We did not have to do it again. It kept right on going and is going better than ever today. Many great exhibitions since then could not have appeared without it."

B. The strongest reaction was to the Cubist Room ("The Chamber of Horrors") and to Marcel Duchamp's *Nude Descending a Staircase,* which was labeled by some newspapers as "an explosion in a shingle factory."

C. One poet described *Nude* for *American Art News:*
> You tried to find her,
> And you've looked in vain
> Up the picture and down again,
> You've tried to fashion her of broken bits,
> And you've worked yourself into seventeen fits;
> The reason you've failed to tell you I can,
> It isn't a lady but only a man.

IV. Impact

The Armory Show influenced a generation of artists (Stuart Davis, Arthur Dove, Georgia O'Keeffe), and as Alfred Stieglitz said, it was responsible for "injecting some life into the decaying corpse of art."

Empathy Sheet

This sheet will be used in evaluating the art slides of decade paintings. *Empathy* refers to feeling, the methods the artist uses to create feeling through the painting, as well as the feeling you have as you look at the painting. This sheet should help to explain the methods, to verbalize about what the artist is doing and what you feel.

1. Empathy in lines or axes of composition

    a. Horizontal—repose, peace, quiet, equilibrium

    b. Vertical—virility, rigidity, strength, static uprightness

    c. Diagonal—energy, dynamic activity, striving

    d. Curved and rounded—ease, comfort, well-being, growth

    e. Straight lines—rigidity and stiffness

    f. Angular and jagged—harshness or brutality, dynamism, brittleness

    g. Serpentine—lithe or languorous grace, suppleness, sensuousness, feebleness

    h. Spiral—restless and exciting

    i. Hard, dark, clearly defined—strength, precision, confidence

    j. Soft, blurred, and varied in emphasis—delicacy, sensitivity, timidity, weakness

2. Empathy in two- or three-dimensional shapes

    a. Simple and regular—restful and quiet

    b. Complex and irregular—restless and exciting

    c. Horizontal rectangle—calm and repose

    d. Vertical rectangle—strength and dignity

    e. Circle—completeness and finality, but also instability because of a tendency to roll

    f. Crescent—vivacious and exciting, especially if the axis is diagonal

    g. Triangle—active, energetic, incisive, abrupt, the most dynamic geometric

    h. Square—sturdy, rugged, plain, straightforward

i. Diamond—active, alert, restless

j. Some shapes seem in themselves overpowering, ponderous, awe-inspiring, insecure, furious, crushing, depressing, buoyant, cramped, brutal, firm, stable, delicate, graceful, peaceful. Mass, weight, force, space, distance, direction of movement, color, and so forth, when added to the empathetic effect of line and shape, create very complex form meanings and define unique aesthetic experiences.

3. Empathy in colors

a. Warm colors such as red, orange, and yellow—exciting, magnetic, buoyant, open, frank, sanguine, radiant, passionate

b. Cool colors such as blue and green—soothing, quiet, inhibitory, depressing, aloof, repellent, haughty

c. Bright colors—spirited, optimistic, cheerful, jovial

d. Dark colors—reserved, serious, somber, gloomy, inaccessible, depressing, aloof, repellent, haughty

e. Close harmonies and monotones—the least exciting

f. Complementary colors—more stimulating

g. By combining colors appropriately, one may express the delicate, hazy, diaphanous, spacious, sympathetic, dignified, contemplative, restless, spontaneous, harmonious, irritable, discordant.

The above are three basic concerns that you will use in your analysis, although art works also deal with empathy in texture and materials, empathy in illumination (such as the use of radiant light or foreboding shade), as well as the expansiveness and freedom one feels in a painting that conveys space and distance. Check off those words that seem to match what you see and feel.

Suggested Procedure and Evaluation in Teaching Your Painting

Make sure that your painting is in focus. Stand beside the screen so that you can be heard and can point to the painting.

1. *The Background:* The name and date of the painting. The painter. The style. If possible, location of the painting today and its size.

2. *First Empathic Response:* Where does your eye go? How does the painting make you feel? What is the story of the painting?

3. *The Three Empathic Elements:* Line, shape, color, which help explain how you feel, what the artist was doing to create that feeling.

4. *The Artifact:* How does this painting relate to American culture, to the decade, to the art world, to the things that you have studied?

Evaluation _____

Comments:

Lessons 46–48 Preparing to Teach the Painting

Goal

Developing a background and method for students who, using slides of decade art, will be teaching paintings as works of art and artifacts.

Materials

1. Handout 24, "Empathy Sheet."

2. Handout 25, which lists all of the art slides available to students.

3. Slide projector, screen, light table or viewmaster, or additional projectors and screens, as well as print material on American art.

4. Resource person: high school art teacher (optional). The instructor should consider introducing the method by teaching one of the slides as a model for student teaching on Lesson 47.

Procedure

1. Tell the students that during Lesson 46 they will be given slides to study for their eventual teaching. They will use the empathy sheet and classroom materials and films to assist them with their preparation. On Lesson 47, the instructor or a resource person will model the teaching of a decade painting.

2. Reassure the students that they will have time and materials for their teaching. Remind them that their presentations will last until Lesson 55, thus giving them additional time to prepare, as well as to work on their projects.

3. Ask the students to briefly review the empathy handout. It will serve as an important guide for their presentation. Note the suggested procedures. Encourage the students to do research, using not only classroom materials but also resources in other libraries. They may wish to refer to their history handbooks as they reflect on the date of their artifact.

4. Show all the available slides, naming each by *number,* not by title or artist. Ask the students to write down two or three numbers of

paintings that they would like to teach. Then distribute Handout 25, listing all of the paintings and art works. Note: Some 1960s artifacts are not paintings, but students may use them for artifact analysis, too. Work with them in terms of ways to present sculpture and 1960s "happenings" as artifacts.

5. Then place the slides, all identified by number, on a light table or viewmaster. Alert the students to the problems of damaging slides if they are mishandled. Encourage some to examine their slides, others to find general research on their artists.

6. Be sure to circulate among the students, checking their choices on a master handout, making sure everyone has a slide by the end of the period.

7. On Lesson 48, the in-class preparation should be completed. Due dates for the student teaching should be clarified. Suggestion: Start the first day of teaching with no more than five paintings to set the model.

Additional Suggestions

1. Here is another chance to encourage collaborative teaching, to involve partners in both teaching the painting and responding to questions from the class and instructor. If the students want to teach as partners, ask them to teach two paintings, both students contributing on each painting.

2. Because not everyone will get to teach his or her number one choice, ask the students to do some large-group problem solving: What is a fair system for getting the painting of your choice? Example: Put the numbers of all the slides on the chalkboard. If only one student picks a slide, she or he gets it. For the remaining slides, let students decide on a technique (for example, a student thinks of a number between 1 and 100, and the ones vying for this slide will get it if they have the closest number).

Handout 25

1960s Art Slides

Paintings

1. Albers, Josef, *Homage to the Square Series: Fall* (1964)
2. Close, Chuck, *Self-Portrait* (1968)
3. D'Archangelo, Allan, *Highway #2* (1963)
4. Estes, Richard, *Auto Graveyard* (1968)
5. Gwathmey, Robert, *The Observers* (1960)
6. Hopper, Edward, *People in the Sun* (1960)
7. Indiana, Robert, *The American Dream* (1961)
8. Indiana, Robert, *The Metamorphosis of Norma Jean Mortenson* (1967)
9. Kanovitz, Howard, *Drinks* (1966)
10. Lichtenstein, Roy, *OK, Hot Shot* (1963)
11. Lichtenstein, Roy, *Woman in Flowered Hat* (1963)
12. Linder, Richard, *Hello* (1966)
13. Linder, Richard, *Ice* (1966)
14. O'Keeffe, Georgia, *Road Past the View I* (1966)
15. O'Keeffe, Georgia, *Sky above the Clouds* (1965)
16. Rauschenberg, Robert, *Tracer* (1964)
17. Rockwell, Norman, *Abstract and Concrete* (1962)
18. Rockwell, Norman, *For the Department of Interior* (1970)
19. Rockwell, Norman, *Moving In* (1967)
20. Rockwell, Norman, *A Time for Greatness* (1964)
21. Shahn, Ben, *Integration, Supreme Court* (1963)
22. Stella, Frank, *Sinjerli–Variation IV* (1968)
23. Warhol, Andy, *Elvis I and II* (1964)
24. Warhol, Andy, *200 Campbell Soup Cans* (1962)
25. Wyeth, Andrew, *Distant Thunder* (1961)
26. Wyeth, Andrew, *Maya's Daughter* (1966)
27. Wyeth, Andrew, *The Patriot* (1964)
28. Wyeth, Andrew, *Tenant Farmer* (1961)
29. Wyeth, Jamie, *Draft Age* (1965)
30. Wyeth, Jamie, *Portrait of Jeffry* (1966)
31. Wyeth, Jamie, *Shorty* (1963)

Sculpture

1. Calder, Alexander, *The Crab* (1962)
2. Hanson, Duane, *Tourists* (1970)
3. Marisol, *Woman and Dog* (1964)
4. Oldenburg, Claes, *Trowel, Scale B* (1971)
5. Segal, George, *The Diner* (1964–65)
6. Wesselman, Tom, *Great American Nude No. 98* (1967)

Happenings

1. Kaprow, Allan, "Going to the Dump" (1966)
2. Kaprow, Allan, "Decollage Happening, Yes" (1964)
3. GUN, "Events for the Image-Change" (1970)

Lessons 49–55
Paintings as Artifacts

Goal

Understanding paintings as works of art and artifacts through student instruction, films, field trips, and other variations and alternate experiences.

Materials

1. Slide projector, film projector.

2. If the class takes an art field trip, each student should make a one-page minimum analysis of a painting (a decade painting, if available), using the empathy sheet (Handout 24) and other techniques employed by the students on the teaching days.

Procedure

1. Review the previous lessons on the Armory Show, the method of analysis, the slide or slides taught by the instructor or resource person. The instructor should do this by showing a few selected slides.

2. On Lesson 49, four or five students should teach their slides. These students will be setting the model. Call on four or five students to describe what they liked about each presentation, as well as ask any questions or suggest ways that future instruction of the slides might be improved. The instructor may share the evaluation vehicle in Handout 24 with these students, as well as evaluate the students. The evaluations should be placed in the student folders.

3. The first few days, build a kind of excitement and tension. On day 51 or 52, the instructor should develop alternatives to reinforce instruction, as well as provide variety needed in this kind of schedule. Consider the possibilities (see Bibliography for sources):

   a. Films: *Georgia O'Keeffe; Nevelson in Process; Norman Rockwell's World: An American Dream; The Wyeth Phenomenon; Andy Warhol.*

   b. Resource persons: The class or instructor can invite art teachers, artists, or directors of art galleries to speak on art and the decade.

c. Field trips: A class field trip can be a valuable and successful experience, because it exposes students to actual paintings, their real colors, textures, sizes—not just slides. It is especially valuable for students to see decade art and analyze it at a gallery. If finances are limited but a gallery is in the community, consider a one-page assignment for individuals or partners. This assignment entails the more direct involvement of students in finding the museum, having more time to explore it, collaborating on a painting that interests them. This assignment should come near the end of the study of art as artifact.

d. Save a slide that the students have not seen, one that could evoke a strong response. Spend part of a period asking the students to respond to it by writing a poem. Ask for the final typed draft of the poem before this section ends. Photocopy the poems and make a class anthology for all the students— an interdisciplinary response.

e. Last day: Now it is time to consider all the paintings that have been taught. Do any major themes or common threads appear in what we have seen and heard taught about 1960s art? Examples: Favorite topics, styles, colors? What is the message about art and life in America in the decade? With the projector, review all of the slides without comment. Then ask the students to do a freewrite and share their responses.

Additional Suggestion

If you have art slides from other American decades, show some of them to provide contrast and to reveal the work of 1960s artists during those eras. Ask the students to do a freewrite about similarities and differences between the 1960s art and those of the 1920s, 1930s, 1940s, 1950s, or more recent decades. Ask the students to develop one theory about the difference.

Lessons 56–70
Poetry and Plays
as Artifacts

The multiplicity of ways in which language can be read and written encourages students to appreciate different perspectives and to articulate their own points of view.

The English Coalition: Democracy through Language (85)

Lesson 56
Poetry as Artifact

Goal

Orientation to poetry as artifact.

Materials

1. Handout 26: "Poetry as Artifact." For this exercise, the teacher should select a 1960s poem and add the first part of it to the handout. Leave room at the end of the poem for the students to "chunk" it (add their own ending).

2. A classroom library of 1960s poetry books and anthologies that include 1960s poems—and period magazines with poetry, if available.

3. The instructor may wish to make a handbook of decade poetry. Eventually, poems from previous classes may be used for an anthology.

Assignment

At the end of the period, announce that the long-range assignment will be a student theme anthology of decade poems. If the students have favorite decade poems or poets, or if they have 1960s books of poetry, encourage them to bring these materials to class for Lesson 57.

Procedure

1. The class will now pursue the concept that poems are American artifacts—as were bestsellers, buildings, films, TV shows, and paintings. Poems reveal intense feelings, often private emotions, that were shared by Americans during the decade.

2. Ask the students to evaluate poems as artifacts. Do the students write poetry? Why? What kinds of people read and write poetry? Remind the students that *poetry* can be loosely defined to include everything from greeting cards and nursery rhymes to famous national poets and winners of the Pulitzer Prize for poetry. Poetry is not just for poets.

3. Chunking: Give the students Handout 26, which now includes the first part of a 1960s poem. Then ask the students to complete the poem in their own words. Tell them they may work individually or with a

partner. Have them share their "chunked" poems with a small group or with the class, opening the discussion with questions about what makes the poems so 1960s in form and content. Ask the group to select one of the poems for the entire class to hear—with a reader and a decade interpreter.

4. Share with students the complete, original 1960s poem and put the poet's name on the chalkboard. Then have the students discuss the similarities and differences between the original poem and their own versions. Use the chalkboard to outline these similarities and differences.

5. Remind the students of the theme anthology assignment. If time permits, they may begin examining the classroom collection. Tomorrow, they will look for a poem or a theme idea that they wish to pursue for their anthology and that they will share with a small group.

6. The instructor may also wish to share a favorite 1960s poem or a tape of a poem or song lyrics that reveals one aspect of the decade.

Alternative Suggestion

You may prefer to continue the small-group approach to learning, announcing that during Lesson 57 the class will be divided into small groups. By day 58, the first small group will begin. Each student must find one poem to teach to the group in the following manner:

1. Give each student a copy of the poem.
2. Read the poem aloud.
3. Analyze the poem's story or literal level.
4. Analyze the figurative or interpretative level.
5. Analyze the poem as a decade artifact.
6. Ask the students to respond to the poem and the way it was taught.

The instructor should evaluate all students on the basis of points c to f above. All of the students should also evaluate one small-group member on these points. Suggestion: Ask the students to evaluate the student seated to their immediate right in the small-group circle.

Poetry as Artifact

What does a 1960s poem look like? What does it say?

Directions: Below is the first part—a chunk—of a 1960s poem. Working alone or with a partner, complete the poem in your own words. Try to make your part consistent with what you believe to be the form and meaning of the first part. Be ready to share your poem.

Chunk of a 1960s Poem:

Lessons 57–59 Preparation for Theme Anthologies and Small Groups

Goal

Preparation for theme anthologies and small-group discussions of literature as artifact.

Materials

Classroom poetry books and anthologies, perhaps a teacher-prepared pamphlet of decade poems.

Assignment

1. Using classroom and library research, find at least five decade poems with something in common: poems by the same poet, poems with the same theme or subject matter. Make copies of these poems.

2. Write an introduction for your anthology, explaining what all these poems have in common. If they are all by one poet, explain what they reveal about that poet. Refer to specific poems to explain your theme.

3. Write your own poem that relates to your theme.

4. Make a cover that ties to the overall meaning of your anthology.

5. Be prepared to work with a partner, sharing your work and ideas, even though you are not doing a collaborative anthology. On day 57: Share books and ideas as you look for poems and a theme. On days 58 and 59: Share rough draft ideas for your introduction.

6. On day 60, you will share your anthology with a small group. Be prepared to give each student of the group (five or six members) copies of one of the poems that represents your work (either your poem or one of the decade poems) and to explain your choice.

Procedure

1. As noted in the assignment, day 57 is a research day with partners, using classroom and school library materials. Work closely with the students, helping them find decade poems—any book that has a 1960s copyright, checking the credits, noting the copyright dates of books that contain individual poems, or poems by poets that were taught or are popular in this decade, even though their poems might have been written in another decade.

   Examples of major poets:

   a. Robert Frost: America's best-known poet, a favorite who read a poem at John Kennedy's inauguration.

   b. Lawrence Ferlinghetti, a 1950s Beat poet whose *Coney Island of the Mind* was taught in colleges in the 1960s.

   c. Allen Ginsberg, hero of the protest movement, who read his poems at campus gatherings and at the 1968 Chicago Democratic convention protest.

   d. Gwendolyn Brooks, the first African American poet to win the Pulitzer Prize.

   e. Imamu Amiri Baraka (Leroi Jones), a poet and playwright who vented his anger at the Black condition in America.

   f. Rod McKuen, singer and lyricist whose books of poetry became bestsellers.

   g. Sylvia Plath, a brilliant poet whose novel *The Bell Jar* attracted young 1960s readers.

2. On days 58 and 59, the students should work on writing their preface, writing their own poem, making a cover, working with partners and the instructor to make their anthology. Remind them to make five copies of one poem for the small group on day 60.

3. On day 60, the students must be ready for small-group Teach Day. Directions:

   a. Show the anthology to the group and explain the ideas and materials behind it.

   b. Read aloud the poem that you copied for members of the small group. Explain why you chose it.

   c. Ask a small-group member to summarize the poem and explain what it means to her or him.

   d. Ask other members: What does it mean to you? What did you like about the poem? Is it a good artifact of the decade?

Additional and Optional Suggestions

1. Offer the option of collaborative handbooks: partners work together on one theme handbook with eight research poems, one poem by each student, and one collaborative poem—as well as a collaborative cover and preface. The partners can share their work with the small group, too!

2. The instructor should photocopy model student anthologies after the first year of this approach.

3. For poems for 1960s poetry handbooks, see the following anthologies and collections by single poets:

> Alexander Allison et al. (editors), *Norton Anthology of Poetry*
>
> Stephen Dunning et al. (editors), *Reflections on a Gift of Watermelon Pickle . . . and Other Modern Verse*
>
> Stephen Dunning et al. (editors), *Some Haystacks Don't Even Have Any Needles: And Other Complete Modern Poems*
>
> Lawrence Ferlinghetti, *Coney Island of the Mind*
>
> Carol Konek and Dorothy Walters (editors), *I Hear My Sisters Saying: Poems by Twentieth-Century Women*
>
> Al Lee (editor), *The Major Young Poets*
>
> Walter Lowenfels (editor), *The Writing on the Wall: 108 American Protest Poems*
>
> Edward Leuders and Primus St. John, *Zero Makes Me Hungry*
>
> Rod McKuen, *Listen to the Warm*
>
> Eve Merriam, *The Nixon Poems*
>
> James Miller et al. (editors), *The Lyric Potential*
>
> Norman Holmes Pearson (editor), *Decade*
>
> Sylvia Plath, *Ariel*
>
> Dudley Randall (editor), *The Black Poets*

Lesson 60
Small-Group Teach Day

Goal

Individual and small-group sharing of theme anthologies, as well as analysis of poetry as literature and artifact.

Materials

1. Theme anthologies.
2. Five or six copies of one poem from the student anthology.

Procedure

1. Review the theme anthology process: finding a theme, developing an anthology, making five copies, and now sharing their work.

2. Ask the students to form their own groups of five or six. Remind them of the procedure for each student:

    a. Show your anthology and explain the idea behind it.

    b. Distribute one poem; explain why you chose it.

    c. Ask another student to summarize the poem and to explain what it means to him or her.

    d. Ask other members of the group: What does the poem mean to you? What did you like about it? Is it a good artifact of the decade?

3. Announce: After each small group has discussed all the poems, the members should choose one poem that they feel is most representative of the group or decade and then choose someone to read it aloud to the class and to explain why the group chose this poem.

4. Collect all anthologies.

Additional Suggestion

Each student is an observer-evaluator of another student and uses a brief observer evaluation sheet to evaluate the person to her or his immediate right.

Observer Evaluation: Poetry Theme Anthology

Name, Period: _____

I. Explanation: What is the idea of the anthology?

II. The student's poem: Why did he or she choose it for Teach Day?

III. Interaction with group: Summary of poem, why group members liked it, poem as artifact.

IV. Superior _____   Good _____   Average _____   Poor _____

Comments:

Lesson 61
Plays as Artifacts

Goal

Orientation to the concept of American plays as cultural artifacts.

Materials

1. Sets of decade plays for small group discussion. Suggestion: *Famous American Plays of the 1960s*, edited by Harold Clurman. Also suggested individual 1960s plays:

> *The Odd Couple* (1966), by Neil Simon
>
> *Summertree* (1968), by Ron Cowen
>
> *Play It Again, Sam* (1969), by Woody Allen
>
> *Effect of Gamma Rays on Man-in-the-Moon Marigolds: A Drama in Two Acts* (1971), by Paul Zindel

2. An anthology of one-act plays, such as *Fifteen American One-Act Plays*, edited by Paul Kozelka, containing the 1960s play *Impromptu*, by Tad Mosel. Or an absurd one-act play by Edward Albee, such as *The Sandbox*. The instructor should consider having two or three small discussion groups on longer plays and one or two performance groups, using a decade one-act play. The performance can be given in the classroom or school theater.

3. "Suggestions: Decade Plays as Artifacts" is an optional suggestion guide of additional plays that can be used as a handout. The text follows this lesson.

Assignment

Each student selects a decade play to consider as literature and artifact, either in a small-group discussion or through performance of a one-act play with follow-up group and class discussion.

Procedure

1. Review the continuing concept of cultural materials as artifacts—films, books, poems, paintings, and now plays.

2. Begin with a brief discussion of plays that students have seen recently in the school or community theaters. Were any of them decade plays?

Can any students name a decade play? Why do Americans go to plays, instead of seeing film versions?

3. Remind the students that the 1960s was a period of intense experimentation, a period of stiff competition with television. The 1960s plays, especially those on Broadway, experimented with nudity, no curtains, open scripts, interaction with the audience, plays held in parks and in the streets. Ask the students to theorize about such experimentation. (See "1960s Theater: Background Notes." Text follows this lesson.)

4. The instructor may wish to summarize a 1960s play, such as *Hair*, and an experimental technique, such as the Theater of the Absurd. Invite the school's drama teacher or a member of the community theater to take part in this introductory lesson.

5. Describe the assignment and the responsibilities of the small group or the performance group:

    a. *Small group:* This group, which will have a chair, a secretary-recorder, and an observer, will seek consensus on three points: (1) the plot: arrive at a basic plot summary of eight or more sentences; (2) specific values and artifact references: a list of at least eight specifics that reflect the decade; (3) one consensus sentence: What does the artifact say about the decade?

      This group must bring notes on these three points. The instructor also may wish to include a group grade to average with the individual performance.

      Option: Instead of the above note-taking procedure, ask the students to make a reading/writing journal where they read and respond to each scene or act in terms of what they learn and feel about the play. They also can be told that during the discussion they will work together on the three points listed above, and they will turn in their journals a day after the discussion, making a final entry on how they felt about their small group.

    b. *Performance group:* This group will perform a one-act play with scripts, either in the classroom or in the school theater. The group members decide on the roles and the staging, as well as choose a member to introduce the play. At the end of the performance, they discuss the play as a decade artifact, also reflecting on the meaning and values of their particular character.

6. The instructor should review the basic plot lines of the plays and then take volunteers for each group or play. Due dates can be assigned later on the basis of the length and difficulty of individual plays, as well as such problems as reserving the school theater.

1960s Theater: Background Notes   Handout

During the 1960s, Broadway found that producing plays had become very expensive and that television provided serious competition for its audiences. The same play that had run before World War II for $5,000 now cost more than $110,000, as was the case of a revival of a William Saroyan play. Backers became jittery when they discovered that only one in four Broadway plays broke even financially. So the 1960s became more and more a time for safe plays by well-known playwrights such as Arthur Miller or Tennessee Williams, or for musicals such as *Hello, Dolly!, My Fair Lady,* and *The Sound of Music.*

But the 1960s also was a time for change, especially Off-Broadway and Off-Off-Broadway. Experimental plays appeared in Greenwich Village, in lofts, small theaters, and even apartments in New York City. New plays and theater groups appeared throughout the country—on college campuses, in community theaters, in parks, and in the streets. The new names included Theater of Life, The Living Theater, The San Francisco Mime. New names, new words, new plays of the 1960s: Julian Beck and Edward Albee; Absurd and Guerrilla Theater; *The Zoo Story, Who's Afraid of Virginia Woolf?, Hair, The American Dream, The Toilet.*

The new revolution was often shocking, a contrast to the old "well-made" plays. The new plays sometimes did not use curtains; often they were held in the round or outside in the open air. The rising Black Theater reflected anger. The plays broke the fourth wall, as actors interacted with the audience. Nudity and profanity were more common. Rock and acid rock sometimes provided back-up music.

A symbolic 1960s revolutionary theater was that of Edward Albee, who was influenced by playwrights of the Absurd Theater in Europe. The Absurd Theater stressed the following changes: (1) Images can replace plot. (2) Audiences can participate, as well as watch. (3) Purposeful action directly written into the script can become just activity. (4) Instead of themes, there may be no set meaning. (5) There is no distinct stage. (6) The script may become an open scenario. (7) A single focus may be replaced by multiple viewpoints. (8) There may be no clear-cut ending. (9) If life is senseless and absurd, then plays may reflect this. Humans in plays may be attempting to make some sense of a senseless world. The plot may at first seem weird, unreal, but deeper meanings are there.

Suggestions: Decade Plays as Artifacts

1960 *The Best Man,* by Gore Vidal
*Oh Dad, Poor Dad, Mama's Hung You in the Closet and I'm Feelin'
So Bad,* by Arthur Kopit
The Sandbox, by Edward Albee
All the Way Home, by Tad Mosel

1961 *Night of the Iguana,* by Tennessee Williams
The American Dream, by Edward Albee

1962 *Who's Afraid of Virginia Woolf?,* by Edward Albee
How to Succeed in Business Without Really Trying, by Frank
Loesser and Abe Burrows

1963 *Hello, Dolly!,* by Michael Stewart and Jerry Herman

1964 *Blues for Mister Charlie,* by James Baldwin
In White America, by Martin B. Duberman
After the Fall, by Arthur Miller
The Toilet, by Leroi Jones

1965 *The Subject Was Roses,* by Frank Gilroy

1966 *The Odd Couple,* by Neil Simon
A Delicate Balance, by Edward Albee

1967 *You're a Good Man, Charlie Brown,* by Clark Gesner

1968 *Plaza Suite,* by Neil Simon
I Never Sang for My Father, by Robert Anderson
The Great White Hope, by Howard Sackler

1969 *Indians,* by Arthur Kopit
1776, by Peter Stone and Sherman Edwards

1970 *The Effect of Gamma Rays on Man-in-the-Moon Marigolds,* by Paul
Zindel
No Place to Be Somebody, by Charles Gordone

Lessons 62–67
Plays as Artifacts

Goal

Understanding and appreciating American decade plays as works of literature and as artifacts through preparation, small-group discussion, and readers' theater.

Materials

1. Copies of decade plays for group discussion and performance.

2. Films or resource persons to reinforce understanding and appreciation.

3. Small-group procedures (see Lesson 61), which may be the design for instructor and observer evaluation of the group and individual members.

Procedure

1. Review the previous discussion of artifacts. Note the assignment and schedule of due dates for small-group discussions and performances.

2. The performance group must have a stage manager, who may also serve as actor.

3. Students should be reminded that when they are not performing or in small-group discussions, they should either be preparing for their small-group day or working on the final description of their project, which is due by Lesson 68. Remind those students who are presenting projects to suggest the time required for their projects, as well as any special materials that will be needed, for example, AV equipment, special rooms such as the school theater.

4. Either Lesson 62 or 63 should be used as a full day of reading or rehearsal. The other lessons also may be used for reading, for films, or for resource people to reinforce understanding and appreciation of plays as literature and artifact.

5. During small-group discussions, the instructor should decide where those not in the discussion should study or rehearse. Members of the performance group should be reminded that the last ten minutes of their lesson should be spent on open discussion of their play.

6. The instructor should evaluate the performance group on the basis of their individual and group achievement. The instructor, along with a student observer, should evaluate the small-group discussions, noting marks and comments in the student folders.

Lessons 68–70 The Term Project

Goal

Final preparation and conferences for completing the individual project.

Materials

1. The instructor should have class copies of term project stylebooks or stylesheets on how to write a term paper.

2. Referring to Lesson 26, the instructor should note on the board the Ten Steps to a Successful Project, pointing out that students are now on step 6. Lessons 69 and 70 will be used for second conferences, mainly for those whose final outline needs further consideration.

Assignment

The due dates for submitting the project or for presenting the projects should be announced to the class and to individual and partner presenters.

Procedure

1. Announce the due dates for term papers. Presentation due dates will be determined during the second conference. Collect final focus-progress reports for the project conferences. Assure the students that the ultimate outline is the one that they write after the term paper is completed or the project is ready for presentation.

2. Remind the students that the dancing and music section involves little homework so that they can work on their projects.

3. Conferences will be held during Lessons 69 and 70. (Examine the final focus-progress reports after Lesson 68 and determine which students need immediate second conferences.) Encourage the students to bring notes and rough drafts to class during the next lessons. Check to see if school computer rooms are available for student writing.

4. Lesson 69 should be spent on class questions about term papers.

    a. Review the previous and final steps of the project.

    b. Discuss the final format of a term paper. Suggestion: Make a bulletin board display of a former term paper divided into sections: title page, outline, seven- to ten-page text, footnotes, bibliography—and the evaluation procedures.

c. Share ideas for writing introductions, conclusions, proofreading, word choice (for example, *Roget's Thesaurus*).

d. Discuss footnoting and bibliography, especially the use of *ibid.*, the problem of plagiarism, the difference between the direct and the indirect quotation.

e. The last two lessons should consist of individual conferences.

Additional Suggestions

1. After you have taught the course the first time, photocopy model papers for future classes.

2. Review how note cards can be aligned to a sentence outline with page estimates.

3. Discuss how project titles can be tied to the introduction or conclusion, to their narrowed topic and final thesis.

4. Remind the presenters that they must inform the instructor of any special requirements of their project, such as audiovisual equipment, resource persons, location for presentation other than the classroom.

5. The day before the term papers are due, allow time to respond to last-minute student concerns about format, footnoting, and the like.

Lessons 71–79
Dancing and Music
as Cultural Exemplars

Although introducing students to the implications of multiple ways of making meaning is the main mission of [the humanities], knowing how to understand cannot be taught apart from some issue or text which the course is trying to come to terms with.

The English Coalition: Democracy through Language (29)

Lessons 71–72
Dancing as Cultural Exemplar

Goal

Understanding dancing as a form of cultural expression.

Materials

1. Handouts 27 and 28: "Dancing and Culture" and "Popular Dancing in America—1920 to 1980."

2. Instructional tapes or recordings (or a resource person such as a physical education teacher) for teaching 1960s—or earlier—dances. Suggestion: Begin with the fox trot because it has been popular for more than half of the twentieth century, was danced by older Americans in the 1960s, and has had a revival since the 1980s. It is simple to teach and reveals how the rules and sex roles were challenged by the 1960s dances.

 The early 1960s dances such as the twist involved both individuals and groups who learned simple, basic movements. But most teenage dancing began to abandon rules. Check local music stores for copies of the twist and group dances such as the hokey-pokey and the bunny hop. Also check music stores for a record on the fox trot—"Learn to Do the Fox Trot: Betty White." Converia-Phone Institute, One Comac Loop, Ronkonkoma, NY 11779.

3. Records or audiotapes of popular music from the decade. Often students have copies of 1960s music. Audiotape or disc player.

Procedure

1. Review the previous lessons on artifacts. Then ask the class to consider the question: How can dancing reveal the values of a decade?

2. Poll the students on how many dances they have attended this year. Then focus on a key question: Why did you go to the dance? Focus on two or more students, male and female. Put their responses to this question on the board—everything from socialization to physical touching. Discussion of dancing will reveal dominant values such as individ-

ualism and external conformity, as well as sex roles. Ask the students to name different kinds of formal and informal dances, such as school dances, the prom, wedding and anniversary dances, military balls. Get them to theorize!

3. Distribute Handouts 27 and 28, which review values and reveal decade dances and values. Focus on the 1960–70 era, which involved a dramatic shift in American dancing. Ask the students to reflect on modern dances and values. Suggestion: Interact with the students. Bring up a male and a female to model the elements of dancing—touching, steps, no steps but individual movement. The students should reveal their dances, as well as some of the dances that will be taught during Lesson 72.

4. The first lesson should involve dance instruction—preferably a slow, pre-1960s dance such as the fox trot. This will acquaint the students with the idea of changing values in the 1960s. The second lesson may be used for faster dances, group dances, and value analysis.

5. The instructor or resource person may wish to teach the entire class or to begin with a small group of four males and four females. Using the instructional tapes or decade music, take the students through the basic steps. Then use the popular decade music for at least one full dance. Suggestion: If possible, use open areas such as the gym or stage of the school theater.

6. The value analysis should reveal the following: (a) People learned agreed-upon steps and clearly defined male-female roles in the pre-1960s dances. (b) The 1960s dances were revolutionary—more individualistic or communal, as well as equalitarian. The young had their own music and dances, often very physical, with little touching. The music tended to be very loud, which prevented interpersonal communication—talking. Often the students just sat and listened to the music at dances.

Additional Suggestions

1. Encourage the students to be involved in the teaching. Encourage a project that leads to teaching one of these lessons.

2. This topic might be taught earlier in the course because it develops a closer class bonding, especially when students and teachers dance together. Suggestion: Try the 1950s broom dance variation, where one student dances with a broom until the music is stopped and everyone changes partners—and another person ends up with the broom.

3. Discuss the return to touching since the 1970s, beginning with dances such as the Kung Fu, the bump, and disco. What does this mean? Are we returning to conformity and sex roles? Is this dancing related to the economy, to the political spirit of the time, to the end of the Vietnam Conflict, a swing to the right? Why are some dances such as the square dance identified as being so "American"?

Dancing and Culture

Because dancing is an important part of any culture, we must examine American dances. This involves learning period dances and evaluating them as we have other artifacts. Remember that dances in themselves are open to analysis, as are dances in relation to the total culture and an era. Consider the following points about dancing and culture:

1. Dancing is often related to a culture's major rituals, such as courtship or marriage. Thus dancing often is done with male and female pairs, with the accent on interpersonal, rhythmic, and conversational communication.

2. Dancing can be a culture's effort toward social and group participation and recreation. Dancing can be for all ages or certain ages, for cross-cultural participation (community dances) or for subcultural participation (teenage dances).

3. Dancing may be a way that the culture channels excess energy, especially youthful sexual energy. However, older members of the culture may chaperone such dances and enforce rules of behavior.

4. Dancing may be a way that a culture develops muscles, balance, coordination.

5. Dancing may be considered therapeutic in a culture, an activity to restore injured bodies and broken minds.

6. Dancing may consciously or unconsciously reveal the values and attitudes of an era: optimism or pessimism, affluence or depression, conformity or nonconformity, equality or individuality, inner-directedness or other-directedness.

7. Dancing is related to the physical environment, outside or inside, private or public, the largeness or the smallness, the lighting or the lack of it. Example: A well-lighted wedding dance versus a teenage dance with strobe lights.

8. Dancing is related to the rhythms and volume of the music. Example: A slow dance with low-volume instrumental music that allows conversation between the dancers and a fast dance with high-volume electronic music that prevents verbal communication.

Popular Dancing in America—1920 to 1980

Handout
28

Characteristics	Slow Dances	Fast Dances	Folk Dances
1920–30 Affluence, youth revolution, rising nonconformity	Waltz Fox trot	Charleston	Square dance
1930–40 Depression, beginning of World War II	Two-step Fox trot	Lambeth walk, lindy, jitterbug, big apple	Square dance
1940–50 World War II, rising affluence, atomic bomb	Fox trot	Mambo, tango, rumba, bunny hop (sock hops)	Square dance
1950–60 Age of conformity, affluence, Korean War	Fox trot	The bop, hand jive, the stroll, rock'n'roll, circle frug, calypso, twist	Square dance
1960–70 Affluence, Vietnam Conflict, youth revolution, civil and individual rights	Early 1960s: bird, swim, mashed potato, boogie, watusi, jerk, monkey. Decline in dance steps, sex roles. Decline of formals, proms, school dances, record dances. Group dancing, individual dancing. More listening to groups of musicians.		
1970–80 Vietnam Conflict ends, Watergate, "me generation"	Gradual return to partners, touching: hustle, Kung Fu, bump. From disco to disco sucks.		

Lesson 73
Music as a Cultural Exemplar

Goal

Orientation to the concept that music is also a form of cultural expression.

Materials

1. Handouts 29 and 30: "Survey of 1960s Music" and "Music as Artifact: Small-Group Presentations."

2. Audiovisual aids for introductory discussion of decade music. See Bibliography.

3. Or a school-made tape and lyrics handout or transparency for overhead projection of one very popular song from each of the 1920s, 1930s, 1945–60, and 1960s time periods. Note: Do not put the lyrics in chronological order or identify the decade for the lyrics!

Procedure

1. Review previous lessons on the concept of artifacts and cultural expression, such as in dancing.

2. Initiate a discussion of the question: How is music part of the culture? Ask the students to name favorite contemporary and past music, songs, artists. Ask them about the favorite music of their relatives and friends. What makes people need music? Why does some music remain popular for a long time in America while other kinds seem to disappear with each generation?

3. Note that this unit, although enjoyable, will not seriously interfere with student preparation of the final project.

4. Distribute Handouts 29 and 30, first noting the general survey of the decade. Ask the students if any of the material is familiar. Note the great variety.

5. Then focus on the lyrics handout or transparency. Ask the students: Which song or songs come from the 1960s? Ask the students to do a brief freewrite on the song or songs that they have chosen. Then poll the class, writing the vote on the board beside each title. Call on individual students to explain their choices.

Note: At this point the students have only seen the lyrics. Now play the tape so that they can hear the decade sounds, the music, the mood, the arrangements, the instruments, the voices. When this is completed, ask the students again to vote—and explain their reasons if they have changed their minds. Announce the dates of each song, review the student answers, replay the decade song, and provide any final background.

Suggested songs and lyrics:

1920s: "My Blue Heaven" (1927). Note the accent on the family, on the home, a happy time before the crash of 1929.

1930s: "September Song" (1938). Note the words "we haven't got time" as Americans become more concerned about being involved in a European war with the rise of Hitler.

1945–60: "Wake Up Little Suzy" (1959). The "Age of the Teenagers" has arrived—with cars and drive-ins and a concern for their "reputation."

1960s: "Everybody's Talkin' " (1969). This theme song of the film *Midnight Cowboy* suggests a concern for individual freedom, only two years after the rise of the hippie.

Additional Suggestions

1. Ask the students for assistance with the upcoming assignment. Do they have any decade recordings or sheet music that they can share with the class and their small groups?

2. If any students have a music term project, encourage them to present their work during this section.

3. Consider inviting school and community resource people to assist small groups, to instruct or perform.

Survey of 1960s Music

The 1960s was an era of change in the presentation and packaging of popular music. During the 1950s and early 1960s, great emphasis was placed upon hit potential of the 45 RPM single. However, by 1965 the long play (LP) had become the primary medium for recording performance of rock music, and to a lesser extent, soul music.

Steve Propes, *Golden Oldies*

Important Events and Experiments

1960: Disc jockeys are threatened with prison terms over "Payola" scandal.

1961: Pete Seeger composes "Where Have All the Flowers Gone."

1962: "We Shall Overcome" becomes a powerful protest song.

1963: Bob Dylan and Joan Baez lead U.S. revival of folk music.

1964: Beatlemania sweeps the nation.

1965: Rolling Stones and the Grateful Dead attract national attention.

1966: Duke Ellington composes "In the Beginning God."

1967: Dolby develops a system to eliminate background noise in recordings.

1968: Off-Off Broadway *Hair* is called "first tribal-love-rock musical."

1969: Woodstock festival attracts 300,000 near Bethel, New York.

Dominant Themes in Recordings

Dance records: "Hully Gully," "Twist," "The Watusi"

Summer lifestyle: "Surfin'," "Groovin'"

Nonviolent rebellion: "Leader of the Pack," "He Hit Me"

Implied sex-drugs: "Stoned," "Day Tripper," "Yellow Submarine"

Rebellion: "Street Fighting Man," "My Generation," "Nowhere Man"

Unity and solidarity: "Why Don't They Understand?," "No Man Is an Island"

Civil rights: "I've Been Trying," "Amen," "I Believe I'm Gonna Make It"

Explicit sex-drugs: "Let's Spend the Night Together," "Light My Fire"

Introspective protest: "The Unknown Soldier," "Give Peace a Chance"

Social consciousness: "Don't Be a Drop-Out," "Love Child," "U.S. Male"

Rock lifestyle: "So You Want to Be a Rock and Roll Star"

Names

Rhythm and blues, early: Ray Charles, Ben E. King, The Drifters, Little Anthony and the Imperials, Four Seasons, Vibrations, Isley Brothers

Do-Wop vocal groups: The Passions, Shirelles, Orlons, Manhattans

Motown: Stevie Wonder, Gladys Knight and the Pips, Supremes, Temptations, Marv Johnson, Marvin Gaye, The Miracles, Jackson Five, Elgins

Southern rhythm and blues: James Brown, Ike and Tina Turner, Joe Tex

Rock and roll: Elvis Presley, Ray Orbison, The Band, Sam the Sham

Folk rock: Bob Dylan; Neil Diamond; Simon and Garfunkel; The Byrds; Lovin' Spoonful; Youngbloods; Blood, Sweat and Tears

California rock and roll: Beach Boys, Rockin' Rebels, Righteous Brothers

British rock and roll: Beatles, Rolling Stones, Animals, The Who, Joe Cocker

British hard rock: Cream, Jimi Hendrix, Small Faces

Latin rock: Santana, Credence Clearwater Revival, Sly and the Family Stone

San Francisco rock: Jefferson Airplane, Big Brother and The Holding Company

LA rock: The Doors, Steppenwolf, Canned Heat

Sample Top Songs for the Year

1960: "Let It Be," "Puppy Love," "Itsy Bitsy Teenie Weenie Yellow Polka Dot Bikini," "Where or When," "Everybody's Somebody's Fool"

1961: "I Fall to Pieces," "Big Bad John," "Pocketful of Miracles," "Michael," "Hello, Mary Lou," "Michael—Row the Boat Ashore"

1962: "I Can't Stop Loving You," "Stranger on the Shore," "Days of Wine and Roses," "Roses Are Red," "Where Have All the Flowers Gone?"

1963: "Sugar Shack," "Surfin' USA," "The End of the World," "If I Had a Hammer," "The Times They Are A-Changin'," "Blowin' in the Wind"

1964: "I Want to Hold Your Hand," "She Loves You," "People," "Downtown," "Hard Day's Night," "Leader of the Pack," "Understand Your Man"

1965: "I Can't Get No Satisfaction," "Sound of Silence," "What the World Needs Now Is Love," "It's Not Unusual," "I Got You Babe"

1966: "My Generation," "The Ballad of the Green Berets," "Cherish," "Born Free," "The Impossible Dream," "Georgy Girl," "Yellow Submarine"

1967: "Hair," "Ode to Billie Joe," "A Natural Woman," "By the Time I Get to Phoenix," "Cabaret," "Light My Fire," "The Beat Goes On," "The Letter"

1968: "Hey, Jude," "Honey," "Do Your Own Thing," "Spinning Wheel," "The Windmills of Your Mind," "Me and Bobby McGee"

1969: "Everybody's Talkin'," "Aquarius," "I Can't Get Next to You," "I've Got to Be Me," "Sugar Baby," "Give Peace a Chance," "Leavin' on a Jet Plane"

Lessons 74–75
Music as a Cultural Exemplar

Goal

Formation of small groups to prepare presentations on decade music as artifact.

Materials—Choices

1. Handout 30: "Music as Artifact: Small-Group Presentations."

Or

2. Handouts 31 and 32: "Music as Artifact: Lyrics Analysis" and "Artifact Assignment and Group Notes."

Assignment Choices for the Instructor

1. Activity committees: Using the handout on small-group presentations, review the choices and ask the students to volunteer for one of the four committees that will make presentations during Lessons 76 through 79.

Or

2. Lyrics analysis groups: Using the handouts on lyrics analysis, ask the students to form small groups for finding one song. During Lessons 74 and 75, these groups will analyze one song and write the assignment. On Lessons 76 through 79, they will assign their song to another group, write individual lyrics analyses on one song assigned to them and holistically evaluate the lyrics artifact papers written by the students to whom they assigned their song.

Procedure

1. Review the previous lesson on music as an important part of decade study.

2. Distribute the handouts that explain the background and assignments of one of the above choices for exploring music as artifact.

3. Ask for volunteers for each of four groups. Each group should then meet and select a chair, a secretary, and an observer. The chair should work with the group in planning strategies and dividing responsibilities.

The secretary should record the names of the group members and their responsibilities. The chair or observer should keep the records and inform the instructor about the group's progress and concerns.

4. During Lesson 75, announce the due dates for group assignments. Decide the order of presentation on the basis of the complexity of a group's topic and the problems with materials and resource persons. Add another preparation day if necessary or provide additional time by using Lesson 80 on term projects as an interval between presentations. Whatever is decided, the due date for projects should be no later than Lesson 80 so that the instructor has time to read and evaluate the term papers.

5. Encourage each small group, helping them with materials, resource persons—especially in the music department—and with reservations of music rooms.

Additional Suggestion

Writing a song in the style of the decade music may have strong appeal to some students. This can be a creative alternative for a small group. Students could study popular songs, analyzing dominant themes and decade lyrics and sounds. Then they could write and perform their song for the class.

Music as Artifact: Small-Group Presentations

Directions

The music as artifact section can be handled by small groups who will present one aspect of the music of the decade. Each group will determine the nature of the presentation, as well as the materials and the location. Each group will have a chair, who will be selected by the group. The chair will assign responsibilities to each member. The group will select a secretary to record the responsibilities and an observer, who, along with the instructor, will evaluate the group.

Note

Each group should consider the following possibilities for use in the presentation:

1. *Experts:* music teachers, students, people from the community, American Humanities students, past and present, who had music projects.

2. *Performers:* students, teachers, people from the community.

3. *Audiovisual materials:* tapes or recordings, films, filmstrips, sheet music, videotapes, slides, photocopies for background on lyrics, overhead projector transparencies.

4. *Group activities:* songfest, group teaching of the class, group performance, interaction with the class.

Suggestions for Grouping

Group 1: Classical or Semiclassical (or Musicals)

1. Instruction on the twelve-tone system, electronic music.
2. Instruction and performance of one work or performer(s), for example, *Hair, West Side Story,* John Cage, Aaron Copland, Van Cliburn, Maria Callas.
3. Compare and contrast decade music with today's music.
4. Select classical or semiclassical music to go with a series of slides—or a light show with decade music.

Group 2: Rock 'n' Roll, Acid Rock, Rock Festivals, Soul

1. Instruction on the history or techniques of any of these types of music.
2. Performance and discussion of these types.

3. Discussion and performance of tapes or recordings of any group or musician.
4. Do a lyrics analysis of selected songs of any group.
5. Compare decade and modern music.
6. Discuss the meaning of rock festivals, concentrating on Woodstock.

Group 3: Folk Music

1. Play old records or modern tapes and discuss lyrics, such as those of protest songs.
2. Arrange a performance with discussion.
3. Compare and contrast decade music with today's folk music.
4. Develop a folk songfest.
5. Discuss and play materials of one performer, such as Pete Seeger, Arlo Guthrie, Joan Baez, Judy Collins.

Group 4: Pop Music

1. Develop a songfest with analysis of lyrics.
2. Play and discuss music on one theme (such as love or war) or by one performer or group.
3. Discuss the top of the charts, best-selling singles or albums, comparing them with popular music today.
4. Discuss musical instruments, past and present, which help explain the impact and feeling of decade music, for example, guitars and electric or electronic instruments.

Music as Artifact: Lyrics Analysis

Your small group is _____

DUE: _____

Members:

1.   5.

2.   6.

3.   7.

4.   8.

Chair:

Recorder:

Goals

1. Find a decade song that you feel is an excellent artifact.

2. Find a recording or tape of the song.

3. In and out of class, listen to the song, copy the lyrics, and take notes on why you feel this is a good artifact in terms of the lyrics and the sound.

4. Using your notes on the lyrics, make a written assignment for another small group, and make at least eight copies of the assignment. Give the assignment and a copy of your group notes to the instructor.

5. Be prepared to play the recording on Assignment Day and to make and clarify the assignment on that day.

6. Be prepared as a group to evaluate six to eight students' papers on your song assignment.

Assignment Day/Writing Day

On this day, each group will assign their song to another group. They will distribute copies of the lyrics and the assignment, noting the due date, and will play the song. In making the assignment, consider the following:

1. Who is speaking? Who is being spoken to? Are they asking questions, giving advice, complaining or demanding?

2. What words or images seem to be predominant? What is the effect?

3. What sounds, what instruments predominate? What is the effect?

4. What is the overall feeling, the message?

5. Do the words and feelings relate to the time? Do they deal with real events, courtship, the family, love and death, the future? Does the song give advice, demand change, or simply reflect one vision of life?

Evaluation Day

On this day, each member of the small group will read and evaluate all the papers from another small group. In arriving at an individual grade, which will be placed at the end of the paper, consider the following criteria: (1) your group's expectations and notes, (2) the writer's own insight into the decade artifact, (3) clarity, (4) organization and concrete references, (5) mechanical correctness: Were there many distracting errors? The chair will average the grades, place a consensus grade at the top of the paper, and return all papers to the instructor at the end of the period.

Sample: Student Analysis

Lyrics Analysis of "Time for Livin' "

"Time for Livin'" by the Association reflects many of the attitudes and ideas of the 1960s. These attitudes, along with the music and certain Sixties' words, make this song a good artifact of this decade.

First of all, the song's message is very important. The lyrics call for relaxing and enjoying life and not being in such a hurry. They make the point that everyone should take time to look at the earth around us and to appreciate the seemingly unimportant things. The Americans of the 1960s should speak their own mind and say how they feel. Everyone is going to die, so it is important to appreciate life. This message of relaxing in a hectic business world seems to be important in the Sixties.

A closer examination of specific examples in this song reflects the mood, if not the thinking, of the decade. First of all, the person kicks off his shoes and loosens his tie. This suggests two things. First, the back-to-earth movement of the Sixties, and, secondly, the relaxed dress styles. The youth felt that how one dressed was very unimportant—it was how one felt that counted. Then he takes off his watch, again reinforcing the theme of lying back and enjoying life, instead of doing everything by the clock. He also puts away his hang-ups and changes his attitudes.

The Sixties was a time for developing new attitudes and getting rid of some of the social stigmas and rules—like formal dancing, music, clothes. The whole idea of becoming more laid back and enjoying life is fundamental to the hippie ideology. They felt that society was becoming too industrialized and de-sensitized, and they felt it was important to get away from all that—and take "Time for Livin'."

With all these references to new attitudes which surfaced in the Sixties, the use of certain words—such as "hang-ups" and "grooving"—and the new musical style, the Association's "Time for Livin'" is a good example of the new music that appealed to so many young Americans during this extraordinary decade.

Teaching the Sixties by Brooke Workman. © 1992 NCTE. Copied by permission.

Artifact Assignment and Group Notes

Handout 32

Artifact Assignment: "Aquarius" (1969)

"Aquarius" was the number 2 bestseller of 1969—sung by the 5th Dimension—as well as the first song in the musical *Hair.* As such, it is a good artifact of the 1960s. In your paper, analyze the song as follows:

1. What is the message of the song?

2. Use three specific examples of the lyrics and the musical sounds that reflect the culture and values of the 1960s.

3. The paper should be around 500 words or two typed pages.

Small-Group Evaluation Notes

1. The song reflects the idealism of "peace and understanding."

2. The references to astrology suggest a loss of confidence in the traditional religions, a new spirituality.

3. "Aquarius" makes references to drug use ("crystal revelation") and mysticism ("Golden living dreams of visions").

4. The song's values are strong on sympathy, trust, understanding, peace, and individuality—and liberation.

5. The song has sounds of Indian instruments, even chanting, suggesting the Beatles' interest (especially George Harrison's) in Eastern religion and music. (Give special credit if the writer mentions the film *Easy Rider* with its references to Aquarius, drugs, and mystical experience.)

Lessons 76–79
Music as a Cultural Exemplar

Goal

Small-group activities and presentations of decade music that reveal the nature of period music and cultural values.

Materials

Assist the group in arranging and preparing materials, as well as securing resource people and rooms, for their activities.

Assignment

1. Each activity group will present its topic during one lesson period. Group members should encourage discussion and written response to their activities. Each student should have a responsibility in planning and presenting the group's particular focus on decade music.

2. The lyrics groups will assign their songs to each other on the same day. Later, they will holistically evaluate the writings from the group.

Procedure

1. Each small group determines its own materials and procedure. Due dates for activity committee presentations should be established and announced. Due dates for assigning lyrics analyses, for writing lyrics papers, and for evaluating these papers should be announced.

2. The instructor is advised to consider an alternative lesson if any group cannot present its material or topic because of unforeseen circumstances, such as the unavailabilty of resource persons at the last minute or student illness. Suggestion: audiovisual material. Or the instructor might develop a lesson on decade music. Example: trace the development of folk-protest music from Woody Guthrie to Pete Seeger to Bob Dylan and Arlo Guthrie with tapes or recordings. Or focus on one 1960s album such as "Alice's Restaurant" by Arlo Guthrie.

3. Remind the students of term project papers and presentation due dates. Write the schedule on the board to generate interest.

Lessons 80–90
Conclusion

After all, it is only when we teachers engage in reflection or what we want to learn and why, only when we "take responsibility for our own meanings," that we become models of what we want our students to become. Only if we lead our students to take such active responsibility will they become full participants in the political and cultural life they will meet after they leave our care.

The English Coalition: Democracy through Language (xii)

Lesson 80
Term Papers

Goal

Collecting and discussing the term papers.

Materials: None

Procedure

1. Before collecting the term papers, give the students ten minutes to do some final proofreading—and correcting in ink.

2. You might also ask the students to announce their titles so that everyone can hear the variety of subjects. Note that in a final lesson students can hear more about the papers of their classmates. Or, at this point, ask the students to note the titles and subjects and learn more about those term papers that interest them. You may prefer to select the ten best papers after reading them, and ask the students to pick any four or five of them to hear about. With titles on the board, the choice would deal less in personalities and more in content and interest.

3. Encourage an open discussion of successes and difficulties with term papers.

4. Or consider this a floating lesson and discuss these things when papers are returned.

5. Whatever the use of the period, *the term papers should be collected during this lesson,* or even before.

Lessons 81–85 Student Project Presentations

Goal

Presentation of student projects and class discussion.

Materials

The students and the instructor should work together on arranging materials and locations for the presentations.

Procedure

1. The students will determine the procedure for presentation, as well as encourage class discussion when the project presentation is completed.

2. The instructor, noting the student responses in the discussion, will evaluate the presentations, discuss them with each student, and place marks and comments in the student folders.

Additional Suggestions

1. Scheduling five lesson periods for project presentations may be insufficient or too ambitious. Nevertheless, all students should be guaranteed a full class period if they need it.

2. Recognition of project presentations and term papers is an important part of American Humanities. Consider the options: Display the projects in the classroom, school, and community (for example, in libraries); invite school and community visitors; offer exemplary research papers to school and community library collections; contact the media for interviews with students; make slides or videotapes for workshops and future classes.

Lesson 86
Final Test

Goal

Discussion of the final test.

Materials

A box containing large, numbered manila envelopes, one for each student in the class. Inside each envelope is one artifact. See "Teacher Notes: Suggestions for the Final Test," following Lessons 87–88.

Assignment

1. Each student should take one envelope and notify the instructor of the number. This is a final test of methodology. The directions are presented on the "Tentative Schedule for the 1960s" (Handout 1). The students are not to exchange envelopes. Their final test is to be a three- to five-page report to their planet's anthropology society and should cover the following points:

    a. Describe the artifact as to its physical nature.

    b. Describe what you think the artifact is. Remember, the artifact must speak for itself.

    c. Describe what you think the culture that produced this artifact must have been like.

The students can decipher English, though topical information such as names would be foreign to them unless explained in the artifact.

2. The students will be given two lesson periods to write this final test of methodology.

Additional and Alternative Suggestions

1. To inspire the students and to help them focus on this assignment, use one of the following sources: *The Weans*, by Robert Nathan; "History Lesson," by Arthur C. Clark; or *Motel of Mysteries*, by David Macaulay.

2. Some instructors who consider the term project as the final "test" will prefer to use these three days for developing previous lessons.

Lessons 87–88
Final Test

Goal

Student study of artifacts and writing of the final test of American Humanities methodology.

Materials: None

Assignment

The final test must be completed by the end of Lesson 88.

Procedure

1. Review the instructions, reminding the students that these are spelled out at the end of their course schedule handout (Handout 1).

2. Tell the students that evaluation is based on the following criteria: (a) following directions; (b) the quality of the prose—clarity, organization and support, proofreading and mechanical correctness; (c) the use of the American Humanities method of analysis, of objectivity and the values analysis.

Teacher Notes: Suggestions for the Final Test

General Observations

The artifact should be relatively simple. If it is a written document, it should consist of only a few pages. Objects from the decade are especially useful, because they relate not only to the methodology, but also to the content of the decade. Yet decade artifacts are not essential. What is essential is a basis for students' objectivity, for applying their ability to see values in an artifact. Try to find a large variety. Be sure that the artifacts are American.

Suggestions

1. Two pages from a novel
2. A short-short story
3. Two photographs
4. Two slides

 5. A tape or recording
 6. A holiday greeting card
 7. A school grade report form
 8. A section of the school's creative writing magazine
 9. Sports cards, e.g., baseball, football, basketball
10. A page from a comic book
11. A short children's book
12. Two valentines
13. An item of clothing, such as a T-shirt with words or a design
14. A guidebook for raising an animal
15. A car license plate
16. A crushed Coke can
17. A candy bar or wrapper
18. An empty package of cigarettes
19. An envelope with a personal letter
20. The front cover of a magazine
21. The front cover of *Time* magazine's "Person of the Year" issue
22. Two ads from a magazine
23. A poster
24. A column, such as "Dear Abby," torn from a magazine
25. Two buttons, such as a campaign button
26. Sheet music of a song
27. A reproduction of a painting
28. Junk mail
29. A sports story from a newspaper
30. Your school's daily announcements
31. A section of the school newspaper
32. A photocopy of a page from a school yearbook
33. A bumper sticker
34. A computer disk or printout
35. Something from McDonald's
36. Three toys
37. A travel brochure

Lesson 89
Term Papers and Projects

Goal

Discussion of term papers and projects.

Materials

Return the corrected student term papers and project evaluations.

Assignment

On Lesson 90, the course will conclude.
The final test will be returned, and the students will write self-evaluations and course evaluations.

Procedure

1. The instructor might use some of the ideas suggested in Lesson 80.

2. Note the activities for Lesson 90.

3. Before returning the term papers and project evaluations, make some general remarks about the term projects. Remember that, for some, this is one of their first term papers, if not one of the first project presentations. And these students may have many more in the future. So teachers should be careful to accentuate the positive aspects, to remind the students that this project is the result of planning and preparation—all factors in future success with projects.

4. In grading, the instructor should consider these factors of inexperience, but should also note that there were points to follow; those who followed them should be recognized. The grades will be gratifyingly high because the whole process had many checkpoints. Refer to the Ten Steps to a Successful Project on the board. Concentrate on detailed comments on the term papers and written and oral evaluations of the presenters.

5. The instructor is advised to spot-check, at random, one footnote. Go to that source used by the student or ask the student to bring that source to class. This will instill in the student, who will be writing future papers, an awareness of accuracy and documentation—and should discourage future plagiarism.

6. The instructor should deal with the following points in class remarks:
    a. Following directions
    b. The American Humanities method
    c. Clarity, organization and support, correctness (proofreading)
    d. The obvious labors of students on research, creativity, limiting of topics

Additional Suggestions

1. Photocopy exemplary papers for recognition and models for future classes.

2. Plan additional strategies for recognizing students. Notify them and the class of the recognition, for example, school and community displays, gifts to libraries, the annual American Humanities Oscar Award. Make photocopies of model papers.

Lesson 90
Evaluations

Goal

Evaluation by students of their work and the course.

Materials

1. Handout 33: "Folder Record: Second Period Evaluations."

2. Handout 34: "Self-Evaluation and Course Evaluation."

Procedure

1. Return the final test.

2. Give each student copies of the handouts on self-evaluation and course evaluation.

3. Ask the students to get their own folders and use them for their evaluation.

4. Comment briefly on the final test, because the students will need the entire time for evaluation.

5. Remind the students to follow the directions and to consider each point on the evaluation handouts, noting the marks and comments made by the instructor and observers on the folder.

6. Note: The instructor should consider the self-evaluation as an important factor in determining the final grade, which must be translated (especially if the *H, S, U* system has been employed) into the grading system of the school.

Folder Record—Second Period Evaluations by Instructor and Observers

1. **Architecture as Artifact: Paper**

   _____ Comments:

2. **Teaching a Painting**

   _____ Comments:

3. **A Museum Painting: Paper**

   _____ Comments:

4. **Poetry as Artifact: Theme Anthology or Small Group**

   _____ Comments:

5. **Plays as Artifacts: Small Group or Performance**

   _____ Comments:

6. **Project: Progress Report**

   _____ Comments:

7. **Music as Artifact: Committee Presentation or Lyrics Analysis**

   _____ Comments:

8. **Term Project: Term Paper or Presentation**

_____ Comments:

9. **Final Test: Report to an Anthropology Society**

_____ Comments:

10. _____

_____ Comments:

11. _____

_____ Comments:

Self-Evaluation and Course Evaluation

Self-Evaluation

Directions

Below is an outline of various points to consider for arriving at your grade for the final period and course. Go through each point and describe in writing your performance. Also note the marks and comments made by the instructor and the observers in your folder. You might even grade yourself on each section in arriving at your final grade.

Remember

If you have not completed the assignments or if they were late, and if you have any unexcused absences, you should not expect or ask for high evaluations.

I. Requirements

A. Architecture as Artifact: Paper
B. Teaching a Painting
C. A Museum Painting: Paper
D. Poetry as Artifact: Theme Anthology or Small Group
E. Plays as Artifacts: Small Group or Performance
F. Project: Progress Report
G. Music as Artifact: Committee Presentation or Lyrics Analysis Paper
H. The Project: Term Paper or Presentation **(Important)**
I. Final Test

II. Your Best Work

Describe the assignment that is your best work. Why is it your best work? What did you learn?

III. Points for Instructor to Consider

A. Attendance: Any unexcused absences?
B. Prior knowledge of materials
C. Outside preparation: What do you feel the instructor should know about your work?

D. Personal factors affecting performance: What do you feel might have hurt your work, such as sickness, part-time jobs, personal problems, workload in another course?

E. Problems relating to the instructor: Do you feel that the instructor has been unfair to you?

IV. Grade or Evaluation: _____

Course Evaluation

1. When you first began this course, what did you think it would be about?

2. Now that you have finished this course, how would you describe it to students who are interested in taking it?

3. This course has been described primarily as a *methodology,* not a content course. Do you agree with that statement? If you do, explain what this means to students who are beginning the course.

4. What did you enjoy the *most* in this course?

5. What did you enjoy the *least* in this course?

6. Below and on the back of this sheet, write any suggestions or comments that would be useful to the instructor and to the students who will be taking this course in the future.

Bibliography

[The Humanities] should include a variety of texts from within the traditional canon as well as from alternatives to it.

The English Coalition: Democracy through Language (29)

Bibliography

This bibliography is divided into three major sections: I. Basic Materials for Starting a 1960s American Decades Course; II. Additional Materials for Classroom, School Library, or Resources Center; III. Films—Other Than Hollywood Commercial Films. For broad categories in the basic materials section, teachers will find specific suggestions in the other two sections.

I. Basic Materials for Starting a 1960s American Decades Course

The interests of the instructor and the school budget will determine materials. Some materials may already be available in various school departments or through public libraries and private businesses. Most of the book materials listed below are in paperback. The instructor of a class of thirty students need not order more than fifteen copies of any book, because the materials are designed for small groups. Other than the handouts suggested to accompany the lessons, the following materials are recommended for this decade course; they are grouped according to the course plan, as outlined in the table of contents.

Lessons 1–10

A children's book or record.

Lessons 11–26

Books

Goldstein, Toby. 1988. *Waking from the Dream: America in the Sixties*. New York: Messner.

O'Neill, William L. 1974. *Coming Apart: An Informal History of the 1960's*. New York: Time Books.

Film

Film or videotape: 1960s history.

Lessons 27–40

Film or Videotape

A 1960s TV program, a 1960s film.

1960s Bestsellers (Select one or more)

Lee, Harper. 1960. *To Kill a Mockingbird.*

Griffin, John Howard. 1961. *Black Like Me.*

Gregory, Dick. 1964. *Nigger: An Autobiography.*

Potok, Chaim. 1967. *The Chosen.*

Angelou, Maya. 1969. *I Know Why the Caged Bird Sings.*

Vonnegut, Kurt, Jr. 1969. *Slaughterhouse-Five.*

Segal, Erich. 1970. *Love Story.*

Lessons 41–55

Architecture Slides

Thirty AV department or teacher-prepared architecture slides: local and national architecture—dream houses, front-rear orientation, eclectic, organic, international buildings.

Art Slides

Thirty AV department or teacher-prepared art slides.

Books

A collection of American art and decade art books.

Lessons 56–70

Poetry

A collection of poetry books containing 1960s poems. Optional: a teacher-prepared collection of 1960s poems.

Plays

Use one or two of the following alternatives:

Clurman, Harold, ed. 1972. *Famous Plays of the 1960s.* New York: Dell.

Kozelka, Paul, ed. 1961. *Fifteen American One-Act Plays.* New York: Washington Square Press.

Three small-group sets of six or seven plays by one playwright, as well as a one-act play such as Edward Albee's *The Sandbox.*

Lessons 71–79

1960s music records or tapes, including one instructional record for the fox trot, the twist, or other dance.

II. Additional Materials for Classroom, School Library, or Resources Center

These materials are useful for students and instructor alike, and some should be considered for purchase.

Books

Albee, Edward. 1963. *The American Dream and the Zoo Story; Two Plays.* New York: Signet.

————. 1959, 1960. *The Sandbox and the Death of Bessie Smith.* New York: Signet.

————. 1981. *Tiny Alice* (1964); *A Delicate Balance* (1966); *Box* (1968); *Quotations from Chairman Mao-Tse-tung* (1968). In *Albee, the Plays.* Vol. 2. New York: Atheneum.

————. 1962. *Who's Afraid of Virginia Woolf.* New York: Atheneum.

Allison, Alexander, Herbert Barrows, Caesar Blake, Arthur Carr, Arthur Eastman, and Hurbert English, eds. 1983. *Norton Anthology of Poetry.* New York: W. W. Norton.

Baker, Mark. 1981. *Nam: The Vietnam War in the Words of the Men and Women Who Fought There.* New York: William Morrow.

Belz, Carl. 1972. *The Story of Rock.* New York: Oxford University Press.

Betty White's Teenage Dancebook. 1963. New York: David McKay.

The Britannica Encyclopaedia of American Art. 1973. New York: Chanticleer Press, Simon and Schuster.

Brooks, Elston. 1981. *I've Heard Those Songs Before: The Weekly Top Ten Tunes for the Past Fifty Years.* New York: Morrow Quill Paperbacks.

Bryan, C. D. B. 1977. *Friendly Fire.* New York: Bantam.

Capote, Truman. 1965. *In Cold Blood: A True Account of Multiple Murder and Its Consequences.* New York: Random House.

Clarke, Arthur C. 1959. "History Lesson." In *Across the Stars: An Omnibus,* 54–62. New York: Harcourt Brace.

Clurman, Harold. 1972. *Famous American Plays of the 1960s.* New York: Dell.

Contemporary Artists. 1983. New York: St. Martin's Press.

Dunning, Stephen, Edward Lueders, and Hugh Smith, eds. 1966. *Reflections on a Gift of Watermelon Pickle . . . and Other Modern Verse.* Glenview, Ill.: Scott, Foresman.

————. 1969. *Some Haystacks Don't Even Have Any Needle: and Other Complete Modern Poems.* New York: Lothrop, Lee, & Shepard Co.

Editors of Time-Life Books. 1970. *This Fabulous Century, 1960–70.* Vol. 7. New York: Time-Life Books.

————. 1970. *Modern American Painting.* New York: Time-Life Books.

Ferlinghetti, Lawrence. 1958. *Coney Island of the Mind.* San Francisco: New Directions.

Fireman, Judy, ed. 1977. *TV Book: The Ultimate Television Book.* New York: Workman Publishing Co.

Fishwick, Marshall William. 1969. *The Hero, American Style.* New York: D. McKay Co.

Foley, Mary Mix. 1980. *The American House.* New York: Harper and Row.

Fussell, Paul. 1984. "The Living Room Scale." In *Class.* New York: Ballantine Books.

Gallup Poll Monthly. Gallup Poll News Services, 100 Palmer Square, 47 Hulfish Street, Princeton, N.J. 08542. Tel: (609) 924-9600; FAX: (609) 924-2584.

Gitlin, Todd. 1987. *The Sixties: Years of Hope, Days of Rage.* New York: Bantam.

Gold, Analee. 1975. *75 Years of Fashion.* New York: Fairchild Publications.

Gordon, Alan and Lois. 1987. *American Chronicles: Six Decades of American Life.* New York: Atheneum.

Gottlieb, Sherry Gershon. 1991. *Hell No, We Won't Go: Resisting the Draft During the Vietnam War.* New York: Viking.

Griffith, Richard, and Arthur Mayer. 1970. *The Movies.* New York: Simon and Schuster.

Hackett, Alice Payne. 1977. *80 Years of Best Sellers, 1895–1975.* New York: R. R. Bowker Co.

Hans, Marcie. 1965. "Fueled." In *Serve Me a Slice of Moon.* New York: Harcourt, Brace, World, Inc.

Hatch, Alden. 1974. *Buckminster Fuller: At Home in the Universe.* New York: Crown.

Hendler, Herb, and James Henry Burke. 1983. *Year by Year in the Rock Era.* Westport, Conn.: Greenwood Press.

Herr, Michael. 1977. *Dispatches.* New York: Knopf.

Hirsch, E. D., Jr., Joseph F. Kett, and James Trefil. 1988. *The Dictionary of Cultural Literacy: What Every American Needs to Know.* Boston: Houghton Mifflin.

Howard, Gerald, ed. 1982. *The Sixties.* New York: Washington Press.

Hunter, Sam. 1972. *American Art of the 20th Century.* New York: H. N. Abrams.

Jarrell, Randall. 1945. "The Death of the Ball Turret Gunner." In *The Complete Poems.* New York: Farrar, Straus & Giroux, Inc.

Joseph, Peter. 1973. *Good Times: An Oral History of America in the Nineteen Sixties.* New York: Charterhouse.

Kahan, Peter. 1980. *American Paintings of the Sixties and Seventies, the Real—the Ideal—the Fantastic.* Selections from the Whitney Museum. Montgomery Museum of Fine Art.

Katzenstein, Gary. 1989. *Funny Business: An Outsider's Year in Japan.* New York: Soho Press.

Konek, Carol, and Dorothy Walters, eds. 1976. *I Hear My Sisters Saying: Poems by Twentieth-Century Women.* New York: Thomas Crowell.

Kozelka, Paul, ed. 1961. *Fifteen American One-Act Plays.* New York: Washington Square Press.

Kunen, James Simon. 1968. *The Strawberry Statement.* New York: Random House.

Lederer, William J. 1961. *A Nation of Sheep.* New York: Norton.

Lee, Al, ed. 1971. *The Major Young Poets.* New York: World Publishing Co.

Lee, Calvin B. T. 1970. *The Campus Scene, 1900–1970.* New York: David McKay.

Lee, Harper. 1960. *To Kill a Mockingbird.* Philadelphia: Lippincott.

Leuders, Edward, and Primus St. John. 1976. *Zero Makes Me Hungry.* Glenview, Ill.: Scott, Foresman.

Lloyd-Jones, Richard, and Andrea Lunsford, eds. 1989. *The English Coalition: Democracy through Language.* Urbana, Ill.: NCTE.

Lowenfels, Walter, ed. 1969. *The Writing on the Wall: 108 American Protest Poems.* Garden City, N.Y.: Doubleday.

Lucie-Smith, Edward. 1977. *Art Now: From Abstract Expressionism to Super-realism.* New York: William Morrow.

Lurie, Alison. 1981. *The Language of Clothes.* New York: Random House.

Macaulay, David. 1979. *Motel of Mysteries.* Boston: Houghton Mifflin.

Makower, Joel. 1989. *Woodstock: The Oral History.* New York: Doubleday.

Maynard, Joyce. 1973. *Looking Back: A Chronicle of Growing Up Old in the Sixties.* Garden City, N.Y.: Doubleday.

McDonagh, Don. 1979. *Dance Fever.* New York: Random House.

McGovern, Robert, and Richard Snyder, eds. 1970. *Sixty on the Sixties.* Ashland, Ohio: Ashland Poetry Press, Ashland College.

McKuen, Rod. 1970. *Listen to the Warm.* New York: Random House.

Merriam, Eve. 1970. *The Nixon Poems.* New York: Atheneum.

Miller, James, Robert Hayden, and Robert O'Neal, eds. 1974. *The Lyric Potential.* Glenview, Ill.: Scott, Foresman.

Morey, A. J. 1977. *The Sixties.* New York: Consolidated Music Publishers.

Nader, Ralph. 1965. *Unsafe at Any Speed: The Designed-In Dangers of the American Automobile.* New York: Grossman.

Nathan, Robert. 1961. *The Weans.* New York: Alfred Knopf.

Norman, Philip. 1981. *Shout! The Beatles in Their Generation.* New York: Simon and Schuster.

Obst, Lynda R., ed. 1977. *The Sixties.* New York: Rolling Stones Press.

Pearson, Norman Holmes, ed. 1969. *Decade.* Middletown, Conn.: Wesleyan University Press.

Pichaske, David R. 1989. *A Generation in Motion: Popular Music and Culture in the Sixties.* New York: Ellis Press.

Plath, Sylvia. 1966. *Ariel.* New York: Harper and Row.

————. 1971. *The Bell Jar.* New York: Harper and Row.

Postman, Neil. 1979. *Teaching as a Conserving Activity.* New York: Delacorte.

Powers, Thomas. 1971. *Diana: The Making of a Terrorist.* Boston: Houghton Mifflin.

————. 1973. *The War at Home: Vietnam and the American People, 1964–1968.* New York: Grossman.

Propes, Steve. 1974. *Golden Oldies: A Guide to 60's Record Collecting.* Radnor, Pa.: Chilton Book Co.

Randall, Dudley, ed. 1971. *The Black Poets.* New York: Bantam.

Raphael, Ray. 1988. *The Men from the Boys: Rites of Passage in Male America.* Lincoln: University of Nebraska Press.

Rose, Barbara. 1967. *American Art Since 1900: A Critical History.* New York: Praeger.

Roueche, Berton. 1962. "Phone Call." In *Point of Departure: Nineteen Stories of Youth and Discovery,* edited by Robert S. Gold. New York: Dell.

Sandler, Irving. 1988. *American Art of the 1960's.* New York: Harper and Row.

Sann, Paul. 1979. *The Angry Decade: The Sixties.* New York: Crown.

Santoli, Al. 1981. *Everything We Had: An Oral History of the Vietnam War.* New York: Ballantine.

Seuss, Dr. 1960. *Green Eggs and Ham.* New York: Beginners Books.

Silverstein, Shel. 1964. *A Giraffe and a Half.* New York: Harper.

Smith, Frank. 1990. *to think.* New York: Teachers College, Columbia University.

Stern, Jane and Michael. 1990. *Sixties People.* New York: Knopf.

Tobler, John, and Pete Frame. 1980. *Rock 'n Roll: The First 25 Years.* New York: Exeter Books.

Viorst, Milton. 1979. *Fire in the Streets: America in the 1960s.* New York: Simon and Schuster.

Vonnegut, Kurt, Jr. 1969. *Slaughterhouse-Five, or The Children's Crusade: A Duty-Dance with Death.* New York: Dell.

Whiffen, Marcus. 1969. *American Architecture Since 1780: A Guide to the Styles.* Cambridge, Mass.: MIT Press.

Whitmer, Peter. 1987. *Aquarius Revisited.* New York: Macmillan.

Williams, Robin. 1960. *American Society: A Sociological Interpretation.* New York: Alfred Knopf.

Winick, Charles. 1968. *The New People.* New York: Pegasus.

Wolfe, Tom. 1981. *From Bauhaus to Our House.* New York: Farrar Straus Giroux.

Workman, Brooke. 1975. *Teaching the Decades: A Humanities Approach to American Civilization.* Urbana, Ill.: NCTE.

Photo Aides and Slides

American Decades. 1971. Five posters, 1930s–1970s. Meredith Corporation.

Pictures of a Decade. Set 7: 1960–70. Fifty documentary photographs on cardboard backing. Listening Library, Inc., 1 Park Avenue, Old Greenwich, Conn. 06870.

Slides of American Housing Styles. William Reid, Jr., Weston Walch, Portland, Maine.

Source for art slides: "Pop Art of the 1960s," No. 7712. Universal Color Slide Co., 1221 Main Street, Suite 203, Weymouth, Mass. 02190.

Vietnam Posters. Ten full-color posters. PFF 104-10. Social Studies School Service, 10200 Jefferson Boulevard, Room 171, P.O. Box 802, Culver City, Calif. 90232-0802.

Records and Audiocassettes

The Beatles: Greatest Hits. Learning Library.

The Black Experience. Spoken Arts.

Bob Dylan's Greatest Hits. Listening Library.

But the Women Rose—Voices of Women in American History. Vol. 2. Folkways.

Contemporary Party Dances. Gillette Madison Co., Box 134, Gillette, N.J. 07933.

Daniel Berrigan: The Trial of Cantonsville Nine. A play of the 1968 draft files burning in Cantonsville, Md. Caedmon.

The Decade of the 1960s. RCA Victor pop songs.

Greatest Folk Singers of the Sixties. Vanguard Recording Society.

Greatest Hits of the 1960s. Arthur Fiedler, RCA.

Great March to Freedom. Detroit rally/I Have a Dream speech. Gordy Records.

Hair. Listening Library.

I Can Hear It Now: The Sixties. Three records, narrated by Walter Cronkite. Columbia.

Joan Baez: Greatest Hits. Listening Library.

John Kennedy: Self-Portrait. Caedmon.

March on Washington. King, Baez, Dylan, et al. Folkways-Scholastic.

Medium Is the Message. Columbia Special Productions.

Norman Mailer Discusses Armies of the Night with Columnist Robert Cromie.
1967 peace protest at Pentagon. Xerox University Microfilm/Cassette.
300 North Zeebe Road, Ann Arbor, Mich. 48106.

The Now Generation Poet. Rod McKuen. Xerox audiocassettes.

Poems for Peace. Ginsberg et al. Folkways-Scholastic.

Simon and Garfunkel: Greatest Hits. Columbia.

The Smithsonian Collection of Classic Country Music. Smithsonian, Washington, D.C.

That Was the Year That Was. 1965. Comedian Tom Lehrer. Reprise.

25 Years of Recorded Comedy. WPR Records.

Twist/Loddy Lo. Chubby Checker. ABKSCO Records.

We Shall Overcome. Documentary, March on Washington. Broadside Records.

Sources of Videocassettes (TV and Film)

Education Film/Video Locator
R. R. Bowker Company
205 East 42nd Street
New York, N.Y. 10017

Video Images
495 Monroe Turnpike
Monroe, Conn. 06468

The Video Source Book
Gale Research Company
National Video Clearinghouse
Detroit, Mich. 48226

III. Films—Other Than Hollywood Commercial Films (Arranged According to the Course Plan)

Values (Lessons 1–10)

America and Americans. Color, 52 minutes. Pyramid.

Humanities: A Bridge to Ourselves. Color, 29 minutes. Encyclopaedia Britannica Education Corporation.

Interpretations and Values. B/W, 30 minutes. Three versions of an unedited *Gunsmoke* program. Cinema Editors, Inc.

Killing Us Softly: Advertising's Image of Women. Color, 30 minutes. Cambridge Documentary Films, Inc.

Why Man Creates. Color, 25 minutes. Pyramid.

History (Lessons 11–26)

America in Space. Color, 14 minutes. NASA.

The Anderson Platoon. B/W, 65 minutes. McGraw-Hill Textfilms.

Dear America: Letters from Vietnam. Color, video, 87 minutes. Ambrose Video Publishing.

The Fabulous 60s. Ten color VHS videos, 60 minutes each. Social Studies School Service, 10200 Jefferson Boulevard, P.O. Box 802, Culver City, Calif. 90232-0802.

Five Presidents on the Presidency. Color, 25 minutes. Bfa Educational Media.

Flight of Spirit of St. Louis and Friendship 7. Color, 24 minutes. McGraw-Hill.

Focus on the Sixties: 1960–64 (MTE). 1965–1969. Color, 58 minutes. ABC Wide World of Learning.

Frontline. Color, 55 minutes. Filmmakers.

I Have a Dream . . . The Life of Martin Luther King. Color, 29 minutes. CBS-TV/Bfa.

John F. Kennedy—Challenges and Tragedy. Color, 18 minutes. Paramount.

The Journey of Lyndon Johnson. Color, 51 minutes. Films, Inc.

The Journey of Robert Kennedy. Color, 73 minutes. Films, Inc.

LBJ: The Last Interview. B/W, 43 minutes. CBS/Carousel Films.

The Making of the President, 1960. B/W, 80 minutes. Films, Inc.

The Making of the President, 1968. B/W, 82 minutes. Films, Inc.

Making Sense of the Sixties. 1991. Color, 6 cassettes, 60 minutes each. PBS Videos.

Martin Luther King, Jr.—The Assassin Years. Color, 26 minutes. Centron Films, Inc.

Moonwalk. Color, 40 minutes. Learning Corporation of America.

Nixon—From Checkers to Watergate. Color, 26 minutes. Pyramid.

Protest: The Assassins. Color, 15 minutes. Pictura Films, Inc.

Protest: Black Power. Color, 15 minutes. Pictura Films, Inc.

Protest: Chicago—1968. Color, 15 minutes. Pictura Films, Inc.

Protest: March on Washington: Resurrection City. Color, 15 minutes. Pictura Films, Inc.

Protest on Campus: Columbia University—1968. Color, 15 minutes. Pictura Films, Inc.

Protest: Prohibition and Pot. Color, 15 minutes. Pictura Films, Inc.

The Selling of the Pentagon. Color, 50 minutes. CBS/TV Carousel Films, Inc.

Television's Vietnam. Color, 116 minutes. Accuracy in Media.

Vietnam: A Historical Document. Color. CBS/TV Carousel Films, Inc.

Vietnam: A Televison History Series. Color, video. Films, Inc.

War at Home. Color, 100 minutes. First Run Features.

Why Vietnam? B/W, 32 minutes. US Navy/US National Audiovisual Center.

Popular Culture and Social History (Lessons 27–40)

America in 1968: People and Culture. Color, 20 minutes. Bfa Educational Media.

Black Has Always Been Beautiful. B/W, 17 minutes. Indiana University.

Black History: Lost, Strayed, or Stolen. Color, 54 minutes. Bfa.

Black Muslims Speak for America. B/W, 33 minutes. Time-Life.

Case Against Television. Color, video, 14 minutes. Barr Films.

The Class That Went to War. Color, 38 minutes. McGraw-Hill.

The Hippie Temptation. Color, 51 minutes. McGraw-Hill.

Hollywood—The Dream Factory. Color, 52 minutes. Films, Inc.

Hunger in America. B/W, 52 minutes. CBS-TV.

The Image Makers. Color, 58 minutes. VHS video. *Walk Through the 20th Century with Bill Moyers.* PBS-Video.

John Glenn Story. Color, 30 minutes. Warner Brothers/NASA.

Last Reflections on a War. B/W, 45 minutes. NET.

Life Goes to the Movies: The Movies Today. Color, 37 minutes. Time-Life.

Lombardi—Commitment to Excellence. 26 minutes. Commitment/Bureau of Business Practice.

Making a Live TV Show. Color, 26 minutes. Charles Braverman/Pyramid.

Malcolm X. Color, 23 minutes. Carousel Films.

Oh, Freedom—The Story of the Civil Rights Movement. Color, 26 minutes. Rediscovery Productions.

Oh! Woodstock. Color, 26 minutes. Films, Inc.

On the Road with Charles Kuralt. Color, 27 minutes. CBS-TV/Bfa.

Saul Alinsky Went to War. B/W, 30 minutes. Black confrontation with Eastman Kodak, 1964–67. National Film Board of Canada/McGraw-Hill.

Sixteen in Webster Groves. B/W, 47 minutes. Viewfinders, Inc.

The Sixties. Color, 15 minutes. Pyramid.

This Is Marshall McLuhan: The Medium Is the Message. Color, 53 minutes. McGraw-Hill.

The Weapons of Gordon Parks. Color, 28 minutes. McGraw-Hill.

Architecture and Painting (Lessons 41–55)

Andy Warhol. Color, video, 53 minutes. Michael Blackwood Productions.

An Architect at Work. Color, 29 minutes. Educational Films Library Association/Encyclopaedia Britannica Corporation.

Art Appreciation: Enjoying Paintings. Color, 14 minutes. Coronet Films.

Art for Tomorrow. Color, 25 minutes. CBS-TV/Bfa.

Art of the Sixties. Color, 30 minutes. Bailey Films.

A Conversation with Walter Gropius. B/W, 29 minutes. Encyclopaedia Britannica Educational Corporation.

Conversations with an Architect (Louis Rossetti). Color, 29 minutes. Madison Films.

Family House. Color, 16 minutes. Perennial Education, Inc.

Frankenthaler—Toward a New Climate. Color, 30 minutes. Films, Inc.

Frank Lloyd Wright's Falling Water. Color, 24 minutes. Aims.

Georgia O'Keeffe. Color, 60 minutes. Films, Inc.

Jack Levine. Color, 26 minutes. Contemporary Films.

Jackson Pollock: Portrait. Color, 54 minutes. Direct Cinema.

Monument to the Dream (St. Louis Arch). Color, video, 30 minutes. St. Louis: Jefferson Expansion National Historical Association.

Nevelson in Process. Color, 30 minutes. Films, Inc.

Norman Rockwell's World: An American Dream. Color, 25 minutes. Films, Inc.

R. Buckminster Fuller: Prospects for Humanities. B/W, 29 minutes. Spectrum, NET.

The World of Andrew Wyeth. Color, 28 minutes. International Film Bureau, Inc.

The Wyeth Phenomenon. Color, 22 minutes. CBS/Bailey Films.

Uncommon Places: The Architecture of Frank Lloyd Wright. Color, 60 minutes. PBS.

Literature: Drama, Novels, Poetry, Short Stories (Lessons 56–70)

Deer in the Works. Color, 30 minutes. A Vonnegut short story. Barr Films.

James Dickey: Lord Let Me Die But Not Die Out. Color, 37 minutes. Encyclopaedia Britannica Corporation.

Kurt Vonnegut, Jr.: A Self Portrait. Color, 29 minutes. Films for the Humanities and Sciences.

Long Christmas Dinner. Color, 37 minutes. A Thornton Wilder play for American Humanities. Encyclopaedia Britannica.

Next Door. Color, 30 minutes. A Vonnegut short story. Barr Films.

The Reason Why. Color, 14 minutes. An Arthur Miller one-act play. BFA Educational Media.

Sylvia Plath. Color, 60 minutes. Annenberg.

To Be Young, Gifted and Black. Color, 90 minutes. A 1972 film about a 1960s play by Robert Nemiroff on playwright Lorraine Hansberry. NET.

USA: The Novel: Ralph Ellison on Work in Progress. B/W, 28 minutes. NET.

USA: The Novel: The Nonfiction Novel, A Visit with Truman Capote. B/W, 28 minutes. NET.

USA: Poetry: Philip Whalen and Gary Snyder. B/W, 29 minutes. NET.

Walter Kerr on Theatre. Color, 27 minutes. Learning Corporation of America.

Dancing and Music (Lessons 71–79)

American Music: From Folk to Jazz to Pop. B/W, 50 minutes. ABC/McGraw-Hill.

Anna Sokolow Directs Odes. B/W, 37 minutes. A dance set to music by Edgar Verese. Ohio State University.

Aretha Franklin: Soul Singer. Color, 25 minutes. Bfa/CBS-TV. McGraw-Hill.

Body and Soul. Color, 25 minutes. Dance and music. Bfa/CBS-TV.

Braverman's Condensed Cream of Beatles. Color, 17 minutes. Braverman/Pyramid.

Discovering Country and Western Music. Color, 24 minutes. Barr Films.

Discovering Electronic Music. Color, 22 minutes. Barr Films.

Discovering Jazz. Color, 21 minutes. Barr Films.

Kinetasis 60. Color, 4 minutes. Charles Braverman.

Mahalia Jackson—Got To Tell It. Color, 11 minutes. Coronet Instructional Films.

Oh! Woodstock. Color, 26 minutes. Films, Inc.

Rock: The Beat Goes On. Color, 20 minutes. Encyclopaedia Britannica.

Sound or Unsound. Color, 57 minutes. Technology changes music. Time-Life.

USA: Composer—The American Tradition. B/W, 29 minutes. WNDT-TV/NET.

USA: Dance—In Search of "Lovers." B/W, 29 minutes. A 1966 production. NET.

USA: Dance—New York City Ballet. B/W, 30 minutes. NET.

Author

Brooke Workman is instructor of English and humanities and a supervisor of student teachers at West High School in Iowa City, Iowa. He has had more than thirty years of experience in the teaching of English at the junior high and high school levels. His publications include numerous journal articles, book reviews, and *Teaching the Decades: A Humanities Approach to American Civilization* (NCTE, 1975) and *Writing Seminars in the Content Area: In Search of Hemingway, Salinger, and Steinbeck* (NCTE, 1983). Workman holds a Ph.D. degree in American civilization from the University of Iowa.